What Women Won't Do

By

Ronald Jessy Coleman

ISBN 1-4033-3251-7 (e-book)
ISBN: 1-4033-3252-5 (Paperback)

This book is printed on acid free paper.

1st Books - rev. 08/16/02

"I DEDICATED THIS BOOK"

TO MY THREE SISTERS AND MY MOTHER IF IT WASN'T FOR THEM SHOWING ME AT

AN EARLY AGE WHAT WOMEN WERE REALLY LIKE. I MIGHT HAVE NEVER KNOWN!!!!

INTRODUCTION

THIS BOOK CONTAINS THE
UNSPOKEN TRUTH ABOUT WOMEN
SECRETS ONLY KNOWN BY A FEW.
IT WAS WRITTEN AFTER VIEWING
SOME TALK SHOWS THAT WERE
SHOWING ALL THE NEGATIVE
POINTS ABOUT MEN.
I WATCHED FOR THREE DAYS AND
KEPT WAITING FOR THE OTHER SIDE
OF THE COIN TO SHOW UP. IT NEVER
DID.
A LOT OF MEN WILL RELATE TO
SOME OF THE STORIES, SOME WON'T
BELIEVE SOME OF IT. THOSE THAT
DON'T BELIEVE SHOULD READ IT AT
LEAST TWICE, IF NOT MORE.

ANY WOMAN THAT READS THIS
BOOK SHOULD TRY TO CHANGE HER
WAYS BEFORE SHE BECOMES A
CHAPTER FOUR OR FIVE.
ONLY BAD GIRLS WOULD READ
THIS BOOK OR THEIR JUST THE NOSY
ONES.
I BELIEVE WE AS A NATION UNDER
GOD SHOULD TRY AND LIVE THE
LIFE THAT WOULD BEST SUIT THE
FUTURE AND THE FUTURE DEPENDS
ON THE CHILDREN WE RAISE NOW.
THE CHILDREN ARE THE
FORGOTTEN ONES, FORGOTTEN SO A
WOMAN CAN PURSUE A CAREER.
FORGETTING THAT RAISING THAT
CHILD IS A CAREER. NOW IS WHEN
THE CHILDREN NEED SOMEONE TO
BE HOME WITH THEM AS THEY

GROW SO YOU MIGHT INSTILL SOME OF YOUR CHARACTER INTO THEM BEFORE THEY ARE INFLUENCED BY OTHER PEOPLE.

NOW HERE'S THE STORY OF WHY YOU WILL NEVER KNOW

"WHAT WOMEN WON'T DO"

Prologue

WHEN I WAS ABOUT 17 YEARS OLD I COULD SEE WHY GIRLS MY AGE WOULD GO OUT WITH OLDER GUYS, BUT NOT ME (US).

THE OLDER GUYS HAD SOMETHING I DIDN'T HAVE .THAT SOMETHING WAS AN APARTMENT. SO THEY DIDN'T HAVE TO MAKE OUT IN A CAR . IT WASN'T THAT THESE OLDER GUY WERE NICER OR BECAUSE THEY HAD A BETTER CAR IT WAS THE FACT THEY HAD SOMEWHERE TO GO WITH THE GIRL. WELL I GOT AN OLDER FRIEND OF MINE TO SIGN A LEASE FOR ME. I WASN'T GOING TO LET ONE MORE GIRL SLIP THOUGH MY FINGERS.

I RENTED A HOUSE WITH 5
BEDROOMS AND GOT THREE OTHER
GUYS TO GO IN WITH ME TO COVER
THE RENT AND OTHER EXPENSES.
NOW IF YOUR PAYING ATTENTION
YOU WOULD HAVE NOTICE THAT
THE TOTAL NUMBER IS FOUR AND
THE NUMBER OF BEDROOMS WAS 5.
THE FIFTH BEDROOM WAS A LARGE
TOP FLOOR ROOM WE MADE THAT
THE PARTY ROOM WITH FLOWERS
ON THE WALL AND THE CEILING
WAS PRINTED BLACK WITH STARS
TO MAKE IT LOOK LIKE NIGHT TIME,
IT HAD A LARGE AIR CONDITIONER
IN IT A WET BAR, A STEREO WITH 6
SPEAKERS.
THIS IS THE PARTY ROOM WHERE
WE WOULD DANCE AND TALK WITH

x

EVERYONE. THE OTHER BEDROOMS WERE FOR US TO HAVE PRIVACY WITH THE GIRL WE HAD TAKEN THERE. SO WE COULD BE ALONE, OUT OF VIEW OF EVERYONE ELSE. AFTER MORE GUYS HAD FOUND OUT WE HAD THIS PLACE EVERYONE WANTED TO BECOME OUR FRIENDS. THIS WASN'T POSSIBLE ALL THE ROOMS WERE TAKEN. THE FOUR OF US HAD THE GREATEST TIME OF OUR LIVES IN THAT HOUSE, NEVER LOSING ANOTHER GIRL TO AN OLDER GUY AGAIN. WHAT WENT ON IN THAT HOUSE WOULD BE ENOUGH FOR ANOTHER BOOK, OF COURSE X-RATED.

NOW I'M NOT GOING TO TELL YOU ANY STORIES ABOUT THAT HOUSE

I'M JUST TRYING TO SHOW WHY I
FEEL I HAVE THE KNOWLEDGE TO
WRITE THIS BOOK YOUR READING
RIGHT NOW.

AFTER A YEAR I GOT OUT OF
SCHOOL. I GOT A JOB AT HALLS
MOTOR FREIGHT COMPANY, WITHIN
THREE MONTHS I BECAME THE
YOUNGEST SUPERVISOR AT THE AGE
OF 18.

NOW I WAS WORKING WITH MEN
TWICE MY AGE AND I WAS THE ONE
IN CHARGE.

MEN ON THE DOCKS WERE TOUGH
AND THE TALK R-RATED.

I HAD A FIGHT WITH THE
TERMINAL MANAGER AND ENDED UP
QUITTING AFTER 6 MONTHS.

THEN I GOT A JOB AT A PEANUT
BUTTER COMPANY. I WORKED IN
THE KITCHEN PART OF THE
FACTORY FOR A MONTH BEFORE
THEY SHUT THE THIRD SHIFT DOWN.
I WAS GIVEN A CHOICE OF WHAT
JOB I WANTED.
THE BEST PAYING JOBS WERE THE
SLICER & THE DOWNSTAIRS
JANITOR.
THE SLICER STOOD AT TOP OF
THE LINE IN FRONT OF EVERYBODY
AND CUT THE PEANUT BUTTER TO
FIT IN THE MACHINE TO MAKE THE
CUPS.
THE DOWNSTAIRS JANITOR WAS
IN CHARGE OF THE WOMAN'S
LOCKER ROOM (OH LA LA) AND ALSO
THE MEN'S LOCKER ROOM. MOST OF

PEOPLE THAT WORKED THERE
WERE WOMEN, MOST IN THEIR 30'S
.(MY MY MY).
NOW AFTER WORKING WITH
THESE WOMEN I FOUND OUT THAT
THEY TALKED X-RATED.
THEY MADE THE MEN I WORKED
WITH ON THE DOCKS SEEM LIKE BOY
SCOUTS COMPARED TO THE STUFF
THAT CAME OUT OF THESE
WOMEN'S MOUTHS. THEY ALSO
WANTED A YOUNG STUD TO TAKE
CARE OF THEIR SEXUAL NEEDS, AND
I MEAN SEXUAL NEEDS PLUS.
THESE WOMEN USED TO TRY AND
EMBARRASS ME WITH THE THINGS
THEY WOULD SAY.
ONCE THIS WOMAN CAME UP TO
ME AND SAID THAT SALLY WOULD

GO TO BED WITH ME IF I COULD TOUCH MY EYEBROWS WITH MY TONGUE, I SAID GET AWAY FROM ME AND SHE SAID OH YEA, I BET YOU GO HOME TONIGHT AND TIE A BRICK AROUND YOUR TONGUE JUST TO GET IT LONG ENOUGH. EACH TIME ONE OF THE WOMEN WOULD DO THIS TO ME I WOULD GO OUT OF MY WAY TO GET EVEN.

I USED TO LEAVE THEIR LITTLE BOX EMPTY. AND THEN THEY WOULD HAVE TO COME LOOKING FOR ME AND SAY YOU FORGOT SOMETHING AND I WOULD SAY WHAT DID I FORGET AND THEN THEY WOULD SAY, YOU KNOW DAM WELL WHAT YOU FORGOT.

I WOULD SAY TELL ME WHAT? I
WANT TO HEAR THE WORDS!
WHAT I HAD FORGOT WAS THE
BAND AIDS THAT EACH WOMAN
NEEDS EACH MONTH.
IN THE WOMEN BATHROOM
THERE WAS A BOX THAT HAD TO BE
FILLED. THEY WERE COIN
OPERATED FOR 10 CENTS. THEY
STARTED TO SEE THAT I WASN'T AS
DUMB OF A BOY AS THEY THOUGHT.
ONCE I WAS DOWNSTAIRS AND
THESE WOMEN CAME FOR ME TO
TELL ME TO GO UPSTAIRS TO THE
BATHROOM. I TOLD THEM THAT WAS
NOT MY AREA. THEY SAID WELL YOU
NEED TO GO UP THERE BECAUSE THE
OTHER JANITOR WASN'T HERE AND

THE WOMEN WERE PLAYING
BOMBARDIER TO PILOT.
WELL WHAT IS THIS BOMBARDIER
TO PILOT? I ASKED THE WOMEN TO
EXPLAIN, BOMBARDIER TO PILOT
WAS WHEN A WOMAN WOULD STAND
UP ON THE TOILET AND PUT HER
HANDS ON THE WALL TO STEADY
HERSELF AND THEN THEY WOULD
TRY AND PEE STRAIGHT DOWN AND
HIT THE BOWL (WHAT A MESS THEY
WOULD MAKE) WHOEVER THOUGHT
THIS ONE UP. (MY MY).WELL I
LOCKED THESE WOMAN IN THE
BATH ROOM AND TOLD THEM THEY
COULDN'T COME OUT UNTIL THEY
CLEANED UP THE MESS THEY HAD
MADE. NOW THAT I HAD SEEN THEIR

WORST SIDE THEY BECAME
FRIENDLY.

THE FIRST ONE WAS 33 YEARS OLD
AND SHE WAS BUILT LIKE A NAVY
SHIP SOLID AS A ROCK, AN ITALIAN
LADY WITH DARK OLIVE SKIN. NOW
I'M ONLY 18 AND I HAVE NO WAY OF
KNOWING HOW TO TALK TO A
WOMAN OF 33 YEARS AND WASN'T
LOOKING FORWARD TO BEING
LAUGHED AT BY A 33 YEAR OLD
WOMAN.

OF COURSE THIS WOMAN HAD
NEVER TRIED TO PICK UP AN 18 YEAR
OLD AND I GUESS SHE THOUGHT
MAYBE I WOULD LAUGH AT HER.
(WHAT TO DO). SO SHE CAME TO ME
ONE NIGHT IN THE LOCKER ROOM

AND SAID I'M NOT SURE HOW TO PUT
THIS, THERE WAS A LITTLE SILENCE
THEN THESE WERE HER WORDS!!!

WHAT DO YOU WANT AN
INVITATION ON A SILVER
PLATTER!!!!!!!!

THIS RELATIONSHIP LED TO MANY
OTHERS!!! THE ITALIAN LADY
WOULD COME TO ME AND SAY, DO
YOU KNOW SO AND SO AND I'D SAY
YEA. WELL SHE LIKES TO GO DOWN
ON MEN SHE GOT THE HABIT WHEN
SHE WAS YOUNG AND DIDN'T WANT
TO GET PREGNANT THIS WAS SAFE
SEX BACK IN THE DAY. HER
PROBLEM IS HER HUSBAND DOESN'T
WANT HER TO DO THIS TO HIM,

BECAUSE HE SAYS THAT'S FOR
WHORES TO DO NOT HIS WIFE.
SO SHE WANTS TO KNOW IF YOU
WOULD LET HER GO DOWN ON YOU.
SO ON & SO ON. ONE WOMAN
WANTED ME TO COME OVER
AROUND 8:00 P.M. AND SNEAK INTO
THE BEDROOM WHERE SHE WOULD
BE WAITING PRETENDING TO BE
ASLEEP AND I WAS TO SLIDE UP THE
SHEETS AND SEDUCE HER, AND SHE
WANTED ME TO WEAR A MASK.
THESE WOMEN WERE ALL
MARRIED WOMAN, BUT ANY TIME
THEY COULD PLAY OUT A FANTASY
THEY JUMPED AT THE CHANCE.
ESPECIALLY WITH AN 18 YEAR OLD
WHO NEVER GOT SOFT.

THIS AND THE FACT I GREW UP WITH THREE OLDER SISTERS AND WATCHED THEM AND HOW THEY TREATED THEIR BOYFRIENDS, ARE THE REASONS I'M QUALIFIED TO WRITE THIS BOOK.

"WHAT WOMED WONT DO"

THE BOOK WOMEN ARE TRYING TO KEEP OUT OF PRINT.

THE BOOK WOMEN DON'T WANT MEN TO READ OR SEE.

WOMEN DON'T WANT THE TRUTH OUT THERE.

WOMEN ARE SAING IT'S A HATE BOOK.

WELL EOMEN HATE IT BECAUSE IT'S THE TRUTH.

THE TRUTH ABOUT WHAT THEY DO AND WANT, BUT WON'T TELL.

CHAPTER ONE

HOW FAR THEY CAN USE YOU

WHEN I WAS ONLY FIVE I
RECEIVED MY FIRST LESSON IN
DEALING WITH WOMEN.
MY FATHER HAD GOTTEN US A T.
V.. SO HE MADE A RULE TO KEEP US
FROM FIGHTING. THE RULE WAS
THAT EACH OF US COULD PICK ONE
SHOW AND THAT'S WHAT YOU GOT
TO WATCH.
BEING THE ONLY BOY IN THE
FAMILY WITH THREE OLDER
SISTERS I WAS PRETTY MUCH ON MY
OWN WHEN MY FATHER WASN'T
HOME.

THE SHOW I PICKED WAS "GUNSMOKE" THIS STARTED AT 7:00 P.M.

MY SISTERS HAD ALL PICKED THE SAME SHOW, WHICH WAS "PEYTON PLACE".

RIGHT THEN I SHOULD HAVE KNOWN THAT WOMEN DON'T THINK CLEARLY. "PEYTON PLACE" STARTED AT 7:30 P.M. AND "GUNSMOKE" WAS AN HOUR LONG SHOW. SO YOU CAN SEE THE PROBLEM THAT THIS COULD CAUSE.

SO EVERY NIGHT MY SISTERS WOULD COME DANCING DOWN THE STAIRS SAYING OK TURN THE T. V. TO "PEYTON PLACE".

NO I WOULD SAY "GUNSMOKE" ISN'T OVER YET!!!! MY MOTHER

WOULD COME INTO THE ROOM TO
SETTLE THE DISAGREEMENT.
HERE'S WHAT SHE'D SAY "LETS
TAKE A VOTE". AND SHE WOULD
ALWAYS VOTE WITH ME. ALL ALONG
KNOWING FULL WELL I WOULD BE
OUT VOTED, BUT MAKING IT SEEM
THAT SHE WAS ON MY SIDE. (SO I
WOULDN'T BE MAD AT MOM.)!!!!
SO NOW I KNEW YOU COULDN'T
TRUST A WOMEN NOT EVEN YOUR
MOTHER!!!! (I WOULD REMEMBER
THIS THE REST OF MY LIFE).
WHEN MY SISTERS DANCED
AROUND IN THE LIVING ROOM
FOOLING AROUND DOING DUMB
THINGS SOMETIMES THEY WOULD
BREAK SOMETHING!!!!

WHEN THIS HAPPENED MY FATHER WOULD COME RACING DOWN THE STAIRWAY ASKING, "WHO BROKE THAT".

ALL MY SISTERS WOULD YELL "RONNIE DID IT RONNIE DID IT". I WOULD TELL MY FATHER THAT THIS WASN'T TRUE.

HE WOULD HIT ME AND SAY YOUR REALLY GOING TO GET IT NOW, DON'T STAND THERE AND TELL ME YOU DIDN'T DO THIS WHEN ALL THREE OF YOUR SISTERS SAY YOU DID!!

THIS ALWAYS MADE ME MAD, NOT CAUSE I GOT BEAT, BUT BECAUSE MY FATHER THOUGHT I WAS A LIAR.

THIS HAD OCCURRED ABOUT 32 TIMES UNTIL I WAS ABOUT 12 YEARS

OLD. SO YOU CAN SEE WOMEN SHOW NO MERCY NOT EVEN FOR A BROTHER, THIS FATHER USED A BELT BUCKLE AND A CAT OF NINE TRAILS. I WATCHED MY SISTERS GROW UP. I WATCHED THEM WITH THEIR BOYFRIENDS AND HOW THEY TREATED THEM!!

ONE NIGHT MY SISTERS HAD BEEN OUT DRINKING AT A BAR, IT WAS LEGAL TO DRINK AT THE AGE OF 18 BACK THEN.

THEY CAME HOME LAUGHING AND YELLING. THE TWO YOUNGER SISTERS WERE TELLING THE OLDEST SISTER HOW SMART SHE WAS TO TELL THE MEN AT THE BAR, (WHO HAD BEEN BUYING THE DRINKS ALL NIGHT.). HOW THEY NEEDED TO

Ronald Jessy Coleman

LEAVE NOW IN ORDER TO GET HOME
BEFORE THEIR HUSBANDS. YOU SEE
THEY HAD NO INTENTION OF
GETTING TO KNOW ANY OF THESE
GUYS.

THEY WERE ONLY MILKING THEM
FOR DRINKS. SO WHEN YOUR AT A
BAR NEVER BUY A DRINK FOR A
WOMAN UNLESS SHE'LL DRINK A
DRAFT BEER YOUR DRINKING AND
NOT THE PINA COLADA AT $4.50 A
SHOT. NEVER HELP HER WITH THE
CAB FARE. SHE'S A WOMAN,ANYONE
WILL GIVE HER A RIDE.

YOU SEE SHE ONLY WANTS THE
MONEY SO SHE CAN BUY SOME PIZZA
FOR HER BOYFRIEND. WHO'S
WAITING FOR HER IN THE PARKING
LOT OUTSIDE.

6

DON'T EVER GO TO HER RESCUE
WHEN SHE FIGHTS WITH THAT GUY
AT THE BAR. IT'S HER OLD OR NEW
BOYFRIEND THAT SHE WANTS TO
GET IN A FIST FIGHT TO TEACH HIM
A LESSON. WHEN ITS ALL SAY AND
DONE SHE'S GOING TO LEAVE WITH
HIM. NOT YOU.

THAT'S THE GOOD SIDE.

THE BAD SIDE IS YOU GET YOUR
BUTT KICKED AND SHE LEAVES
WITH HIM ANYHOW.

YOUR FRIENDS HAND YOU AN ICE
PACK FOR THE BUMP ABOVE YOUR
EYE.

NEVER TAKE A WOMAN TO YOUR
HOME. ONCE THEY KNOW WHERE
YOU LIVE YOU CAN NEVER GET
AWAY FROM THEM.

IF YOU DIDN'T CALL THEM YESTERDAY THEY WILL BE THERE TODAY.

THEY WILL TELL YOU HOW MUCH MONEY YOU COULD SAVE IF SHE'S MOVES IN AND THAT IF IT DOESN'T WORK OUT SHE'D JUST LEAVE. WHAT SHE REALLY MEANS IS PAY MY RENT FOR ME UNTIL I FIND SOMEONE WITH MORE MONEY.

YOU WILL KNOW WHEN IT DOESN'T WORK OUT WHEN YOU COME HOME FROM WORK AND THE OTHER GUY IS STILL IN BED WHEN YOU GET THERE. SHE'LL SAY "WELL I TRIED TO TELL YOU, SO DO YOU WANT ME TO LEAVE NOW"!?!?

NOW THE GUY SHE'S WITH IS STUCK BECAUSE HE FEELS HE

HELPED PUT HER IN THIS SPOT WITH
NO WHERE ELSE TO GO. (MY MY).
THE PLACE SHE SHOULD GO IS ON
HER OWN. SO DON'T BE A SUCKER
DON'T TAKE HER WITH YOU IF
YOU'RE THE OTHER GUY, OR YOU
WILL HAVE THE SAME FUTURE IF
YOU DO!!!!
YOU HAVE WOMEN THAT USE YOU.
YOU HAVE WOMEN THAT TAKE
ADVANTAGE OF YOU.
YOU HAVE WOMEN THAT LIE TO
YOU. YOU HAVE WOMEN THAT USE
YOUR FRIENDS OR FAMILY AGAINST
YOU.
YOU HAVE WOMEN THAT WILL
STEAL YOUR MONEY AND ANYTHING
ELSE THEY THINK THEY CAN GET
AWAY WITH!!!!

A WOMAN'S MAIN INTEREST IS YOUR MONEY. HER SECOND MAIN INTEREST IS AN ORGASM. HER THIRD MAIN INTEREST IS HOW MUCH SHE CAN TAKE ADVANTAGE OF YOU.

WE ARE STARTING WITH THE THIRD INTEREST FIRST.

AT ONE TIME WOMEN WERE THOUGHT OF AS ANGELS OF MERCY, CARING FOR YOU IN ILLNESS AND COMFORTING YOU IN DEATH.

NOW YOUR LUCKY IF THEY EVEN STOP TO PICK UP YOUR MEDICINE. LET ALONE SHOW UP FOR THE FUNERAL.

NOW WOMEN SAY THEY WANT TO BE EQUAL, BUT WOMAN REALLY WANT TO BE MORE THAN EQUALS!!!!

THEY WANT DOUBLE STANDARDS
FOR THEMSELVES.
LETS SAY THE SAME THING
HAPPENS IN REVERSE TO WHAT
HAPPEN ON PAGE (6) WELL YOU WILL
FIND THAT YOUR CLOTHES COVER
THE FRONT LANDSCAPE, YOUR
STEREO LOOKS LIKE SOME KIND OF
NEW ART, ANY PICTURES YOU HAD
ARE IN TWO PIECES, YOUR CAR HAS
BEEN TRASHED AND THE WINDOWS
ARE ALL BROKEN!!!!
HELL HAS NO FURY LIKE A
WOMAN SCORNED!!!!
HAVE A MAN DO THE SAME THING
AND HE'D GET ONE TO SIX MONTHS
IN JAIL!!
IF THE WOMAN YOU MET AT THE
BAR LAST NIGHT LIKES YOUR

APARTMENT. SHE MIGHT BE BACK TO TELL YOU SHE'S MOVING IN AND IF YOU DON'T GO FOR IT!!

SHE'S GOING TO THE HOSPITAL. TO GET YOUR DNA SAMPLE AND SHE'LL TELL THE AUTHORITIES YOU RAPED HER WHILE SHE WAS DRUNK!!!

ANOTHER GOOD REASON TO PRACTICE SAFE SEX (WEAR A RUBBER).

THE LAW SAYS THAT IF A MAN HAS SEX WITH A WOMAN WHO'S BEEN DRINKING, THEN THAT MAN TOOK ADVANTAGE OF HER WHILE SHE WAS IN A DRUNKEN STATE THAT MAKES IT RAPE.

THAT JUST BECAUSE SHE SAID YES
LAST NIGHT, DOESN'T MEAN YES IN
THE MORNING.

SHE'S NOT RESPONSIBLE FOR HER
ACTIONS BECAUSE OF DRINK!!!!

THIS IS WHEN I FOR ONE AM AT A
LOSS FOR IF YOU ARE OPERATING A
MOTOR VEHICLE WHEN DRINKING
YOU ARE RESPONSIBLE FOR YOUR
ACTIONS.

(BUT NOT IN BED)!!!!

THERE ARE OTHER THINGS LIKE
THIS, THAT ARE DOUBLE STANDARDS
FOR WOMEN ONLY!!!!

LET'S TAKE THE MILITARY FOR
EXAMPLE WHEN I WAS IN THE
SERVICE, THE FIRST THING THEY
MADE YOU AWARE OF IS YOU WERE

NO LONGER AN INDIVIDUAL AND
YOU HAD NO RIGHTS!!!
YOU WERE IN FACT NOTHING
MORE THEN U.S. GOVERNMENT
PROPERTY.
YOU GOT A SUNBURN YOU WOULD
RECEIVE AN ARTICLE 15 (ABOUT THE
SAME AS A TRAFFIC TICKET). THE
ARTICLE 15 WOULD READ
SOMETHING LIKE THIS; FINED ½
MONTHS PAY FOR ONE MONTH FOR
DAMAGING GOVERNMENT
PROPERTY.
NOW THEY ARE CHARGING
OFFICERS AND NON-COMS WITH
RAPE I DON'T UNDERSTAND WHY
THE CHARGES AREN'T WHAT THEY
SHOULD BE. UNAUTHORIZED USE OF
GOVERNMENT PROPERTY AND/OR

MISUSE OF GOVERNMENT
PROPERTY.
WHEN YOU USE THE CHARGE OF
RAPE. YOU ARE NOW SAYING THAT
THIS PIECE OF GOVERNMENT
PROPERTY HAS INDIVIDUAL RIGHTS
AND HAS JUST BECAME AN
INDIVIDUAL AGAIN.
SOMETHING A MAN HAS NEVER
HAD WHEN IN THE SERVICE.
WHEN YOU ALTER THE RULES
BECAUSE OF GENDER YOU TAKE
AWAY THE EQUALITY AND THIS
CAUSES RESENTMENT AMONG THE
COUNTERPARTS.
THIS COUNTRY WAS FOUNDED ON
THE PRINCIPLE OF EQUALITY.

LETS SAY A WOMAN IS UPSET THAT HER HUSBAND HAS BEEN UNFAITHFUL TO HER.

SO SHE WAITS TILL HE'S ASLEEP AND CASTRATES HIM!!!! OUCH!!

THE COURTS SAY "TROUBLED WIFE" AND SHE IS GIVEN A LIGHT SENTENCE EVEN THOUGH SHE WAITED FOR THE OPPORTUNITY TO COMMIT THE ACT. THIS WAS PREMEDITATED, THOUGHT OUT AND PLANNED FROM THE TIME SHE FOUND OUT ABOUT HUSBAND'S INFIDELITY.

NOW LETS SAY A MAN FINDS OUT HIS WIFE HAS BEEN UNFAITHFUL TO HIM!!!

HIS REACTION IS TO POP HER IN THE MOUTH.

HE GOES TO COURT AND IS LABELED A "BRUTAL BEAST" AND IS SENTENCED TO ONE TO TWO YEARS FOR ASSAULT.

HE GOES TO JAIL, SHE GOES HOME.

SHE'S LEFT WITH A BRUISE AND HE'S LEFT WITH A STUB.

NOW A DAYS A MAN CAN'T LOOK OR TALK TO A WOMAN UNLESS HE FOLLOWS THE RULES. (their rules) NO WHISTLING, HOWLING, AND NO SEXIST REMARKS.

YOU CAN'T SAY "WOW, YOU LOOK SEXY IN THAT DRESS, I COULD EAT YOU ALIVE."

YOUR BEING TOLD WHAT TO SAY AND WHEN TO SAY IT!!!!

WHAT TO THINK AND HOW TO ACT
BY A WOMAN'S STANDARD. WELL
EXCUSE ME, BUT WE ARE MEN NOT
WOMEN SO LETS NOT FORGET THAT
THIS GOVERNMENT NO LONGER
WANTS TO BE UNCLE SAM.
NOW THE GOVERNMENT WANTS
TO BE YOUR FATHER. WELL WE ALL
KNOW HOW
WELL WE LISTEN TO DAD!!!!
IF A MAN IS GOOSED BY A WOMAN
AT WORK, AND HE TRIES TO REPORT
IT. HE'S LAUGHED AT OR TOLD TO
IGNORE IT.
HOW DO YOU IGNORE A HARD
ON!!!
IF THIS SAME THING HAPPENS TO
A WOMAN, SHE JUST BECAME ABOUT
$100,000 RICHER.

**LET ME TELL YOU RIGHT NOW
THERE IS NO SUCH THING AS SEXUAL
HARASSMENT. MEN WERE BORN
WITH A NATURAL INSTINCT TO
CHASE WOMEN, YOU KNOW THAT'S
WHAT MAKES US HAVE THE DRIVE
TO HAVE SEX, SO WE HAVE
CHILDREN SO THAT RACE WILL. GO
ON.
ITS IN THE MALE HORMONE THAT
MAKES HIM BREED!!!!
A MAN CAN NO MORE STOP
BREATHING THEN STOP CHASING
WOMEN!!!!
IN THE OLD DAYS WHEN A MAN
KEPT SHOWING UNWANTED
ATTENTION TO A WOMAN, HE
WOULD BE CHARGED WITH THE
MASHING LAW.**

A LAW THAT HASN'T BEEN USED IN YEARS, My My.

YOU SEE CONGRESS WANTED TO WRITE NEW LAWS SO THEY COULD GET THE WOMAN'S VOTE AND ADD SOME NEW LAWSUITS TO THEIR LIST OF WAYS TO MAKE MORE MONEY!

YOU SEE THERE ARE SO MANY LAWYERS NOW THEY NEED JOB SECURITY AND NEW LAWS TO GET MORE MONEY. CONGRESS AND THE SENATE IS NOTHING BUT LAWYERS SO YOU CAN SEE THIS WORKS OUT TO BE IN THEIR BEST INTEREST THEY CAN MAKE NEW LAWS THAT AREN'T NEEDED AND WOMEN WILL THINK THEY ARE PASSING THESE LAWS BECAUSE THEY CARE.

YES THEY CARE ABOUT MAKING
MONEY AND GETTING VOTES, NOT
WOMEN'S NEEDS!!!!
SO THEY GET TO KILL TWO BIRDS
WITH ONE STONE, MORE VOTES AND
MORE LAW SUITS FOR MORE
LAWYERS.
WELL LETS NOT GET OFF TRACK
HERE OR WOMEN MIGHT NOTICE
THEY ARE BEING USED IN MUCH
LARGER SCALE THEN THEY HAVE
EVER THOUGHT!!!!
NOW HERE IS A ANOTHER DOUBLE
STANDARD A WOMAN YOUR LIVING
WITH TELLS YOU
SHE'S PREGNANT "WOW" YOUR
FIRST CHILD! NO YOUR WRONG SHE
DOESN'T WANT THE BABY.

JEAN SAYS SHE IS TO YOUNG TO HAVE A CHILD (SHE'S 19) YOU TELL JEAN THAT YOU DON'T WANT TO SEE YOUR FIRST BORN KILLED!!

YOUR DESPERATE, YOU TELL HER THAT IF SHE HAS THE KID YOU WELL TAKE CARE OF IT AND SHE CAN GO DO WHAT EVER SHE WANTS TO!! JUST DON'T KILL THE BABY!!!!

YOU TELL HER THAT IN 5 YEARS FROM NOW IF SHE WANTS THE BABY BACK YOU WILL GIVE IT BACK TO HER BECAUSE AT LEASE IT WELL STILL BE ALIVE. SHE SAYS SHE WANTS $400.oo FOR AN ABORTION JOE SAYS YOU WANT ME TO PAY TO KILL MY OWN CHILD. JEAN SAYS THAT'S THE LAW. (SHE'S RIGHT)

THE MAN HAS TO PAY THE MED.
BILL OR THE CHILD SUPORT AND
HAVE NOTHING TO SAY IF IT LIVES
OR DIES HOW CAN THIS BE JUST?
IF A MAN HAS TO PAY ETHER WAY
THEN HE SHOULD HAVE A SAY IF THE
CHILD LIVES OR DIES!!
WHEN HE TOLD JEAN THAT SHE
ONLY HAD TO REALLY GO THUR
ABOUT SIX MONTHS OF
DISCOMFORT, ISN'T IT WORTH IT
FOR THE BABY? IT'S A NEW LIFE.
"DON'T KILL MY CHILD" THESE
WORDS WHERE NOT HEAR AS IF JOE
WAS TALKING TO A DEAF COURT
AND A DEAF WOMAN.
THIS IS A WOMEN JOE HAS BEEN
WITH FOR 10 MONTHS AND SAID HE
SAW HER WITH OTHER KIDS AND

**HER EYES WOULD LIGHT UP LIKE
SHE WAS TOTALLY ENJOYING THE
KID!!!
HOW COULD THIS SAME WOMAN
HE'S BEEN LIVING WITH HAVE SO
LITTLE FEELING FOR AN UNBORN
BABY, .AND HOW COULD HE NOT
KNOW SHE FELT THIS WAY???
IF A MAN HAS NO SAY SO IN ANY
OF THIS THEN SURELY HE
SHOULDN'T HAVE TO PAY FOR ANY
OF IT.
YOU CAN'T HAVE IT BOTH WAYS!
BUT THE LAW SAYS THAT A
WOMAN CAN HAVE IT BOTH WAYS!
(HOW SAD)
NOW YOU WOULD HAVE TO SAY
THAT JOE WAS A CARING AND
DECENT GUY JUST WHAT A WOMAN**

MIGHT WANT, BUT NOT JEAN. (What happens to nice guys)

NOW HERE'S THE REVERSE SCOTT DOESN'T WANT THE GIRL TO HAVE THE BABY SHE SAYS IS HIS.

SCOTT DOESN'T BELIEVE IT'S HIS, I MEAN THERE WHERE THREE OTHER GUYS IN THE ROOM AT THE TIME OF CONCEPTION.

I HEAR OF SCOTT'S PROBLEM, SO I GO OVER TO CHECK ON HIM TO SEE WHAT HE PLANS TO DO.

WHEN I GET UP IN SCOTT'S ROOM HE'S ON THE FLOOR COUNTING ALL THE $100.oo SAVING BOND THAT HIS FATHER HAD GIVEN HIM SINCE HE WAS BORN, THAT'S 18 YEARS AT ONE BOND EACH MONTH.

HIS FATHER HAD DONE THIS SO SCOTT WOULD HAVE MONEY FOR COLLEGE. TOTAL AMOUNT WOULD EQUALS $22,600.oo, HIS FATHER WOULD ADD A EXTRA $50.oo BOND ON CHRISTMAS (IN CASE YOU CHECK MY MATH)!!!

SCOTT WHAT ARE YOU DOING, I NEVER NEW YOU HAD THESE BONDS, YOUR RICH AND YOU NEVER FILL THE GAS TANK IN YOUR CAR!! (THIS IS A CHEAP GUY) SCOTT SAYS HE'S TRYING TO SEE IF HE HAS ENOUGH MONEY TO PAY OFF THE GIRL "BUSZY" PAY HER OFF,!! (A GUY THAT WOULDN'T SPEND MORE THEN 2 DOLLARS AT A TIME GETTING GAS) I THOUGHT YOU SAID IT WASN'T YOUR KID??

I KNOW COLEMAN BUT SHE'S
TALKING ABOUT TAKING EVERYONE
TO COURT TO PROVE WHO'S KID IT
IS!!

I SAY WILL THEN YOU'LL KNOW
FOR SURE WHETHER IT'S YOURS OR
NOT. SCOTT SAYS COLEMAN YOU
KNOW HOW UGLY THIS GIRL IS!!!!

I SAID YEA I KNOW HOW UGLY
SHE IS MY OWN DOG WAS SCARED OF
HER, HE WOULD RUN UNDER THE
KITCHEN TABLE ANY TIME SHE
CAME OVER. AND WOULD KEEP
HOWLING TILL SHE LEFT.

SCOTT SAYS THAT'S RIGHT AND
I'M TELLING YOU RIGHT NOW.##!!**
IF SHE GOES TO COURT I WOULD
HAVE TO SIT UP THERE AND BEFORE
A JUDGE, I WOULD HAVE TO TESTIFY

THAT I HAD SEX WITH HER, I DON'T WANT THE WORLD TO KNOW I HAD SEX WITH THAT.

WOW I NEVER SAW A GIRL USE HER LOOKS AGAINST A GUY IN THIS WAY BEFORE.

THIS GIRL WAS SO UGLY THAT WHEN SHE STOPPED AT A RED LIGHT PEOPLE WOULD CALL PARAMEDICS TO THE ACCIDENT THEY THOUGHT SHE WAS IN!!!!

THERE ARE WOMEN OUT THERE WHOM IF THEY NEED TO GET SOMETHING MOVED AND THEY KNOW A GUY AT WORK THAT HAS A LARGE TRUCK. Oh Boy. SHE'LL INVITE HIM OVER FOR SUPPER AND TAKE HIM TO BED JUST TO GET HIM TO MOVE HER STUFF.

THE GUY DOES IT BECAUSE HE
THINKS THIS WOMAN LIKES HIM.
(How Naïve). SHE MUST, I MEAN SHE
MADE SUPPER FOR HIM.
SHE WENT TO BED WITH HIM. SHE
ASKED HIM TO HELP HER IN A TIME
OF NEED.
HE THINKS TO HIMSELF {MAN I
DIDN'T EVEN KNOW SHE WAS
INTERESTED IN ME).
WELL WAKE UP BUDDY, SHE ISN'T.
THE NEXT DAY AFTER MOVING
EVERYTHING, HE GOES OVER TO
HER NEW PLACE AND RINGS THE
BELL.
SHE ANSWERS THE DOOR AND
ASKS "WHAT ARE YOU DOING HERE".
DUHhhhhhhhhh!!!!

YOU STAND THERE AND ALL AT ONCE IT HITS YOU THIS WOMAN JUST USED YOU. THANK YOU VERY MUCH.

HERE IS ANOTHER EXAMPLE. A WOMAN WHO WAS DIVORCED FROM HER LAST HUSBAND AND LEFT WITH A SON OF 5 YEARS OF AGE.

SHE HAS A GOOD JOB AND WANTS TO ADD A HOT TUB TO HER BACK PATIO.

UNKNOWN TO HER SHE NEEDS A PLUMBER TO INSTALL THE TUB.

AFTER PAYING $2800.00 FOR THE HOT TUB SHE REALLY ISN'T READY TO PAY ANOTHER 2 THOUSAND MORE FOR THE PLUMBER TO HOOK IT UP.

SOMEONE AT HER JOB TELLS HER
SHE KNOWS A PLUMBER. SO SHE
SAYS "I'D LIKE TO MEET HIM.
LETS CALL HIM MIKE. WELL MIKE
IS AT HIS REGULAR BAR.
LETS CALL THE GIRL DEBBIE. HER
FRIENDS NAME WILL BE SUE.
SUE TAKES DEBBIE TO THE BAR
AND TELLS MIKE THAT HER FRIEND
DEBBIE LIKES HIM AND THINKS HE'S
KIND OF CUTE.
SO MIKE SETS UP A DATE FOR
NEXT WEEK AND TAKES HER TO A
GOOD MOVIE AND DINNER. (That's not
enough she wants the works) DEBBIE
TELLS HIM WHAT A WONDERFUL
TIME SHE HAD AND NEXT WEEK HE
SHOULD COME OVER TO HER HOUSE
SO SHE COULD MAKE HIM DINNER.

SO MIKE GOES OVER AND HAS A NICE ROAST BEEF DINNER AND MEETS HER SON. (Woman will use anything to get what they want. even a small child.) AFTER DINNER DEBBIE TAKES MIKE OUT TO THE BACK YARD AND MIKE ASKS WHAT'S WITH THE HOT TUB SITTING THERE. DEBBIE TELLS HIM HOW SHE BOUGHT IT AND NO ONE TOLD HER SHE WOULD NEED A PLUMBER TO INSTALL IT, AND LIVING ALONE WITH HER SON SHE COULDN'T AFFORD THE ADDED COST.

HER SON TELLS MIKE HOW HE IS LOOKING FORWARD TO JUMPING IN IT.

UH OH, MIKE IS BUYING IT, AND TELLS DEBBIE THAT HE HAS THE

TIME AND THE STUFF SHE NEEDS
AND HE'D BE HAPPY TO HELP HER
OUT. (At no cost.) SO DEBBIE IS SO
HAPPY SHE TAKES MIKE TO BED
TELLING HIM HOW WONDERFUL HE
IS.

IT ONLY TAKES MIKE ABOUT 3
HOURS TO PUT THE WHOLE THING
TOGETHER AND DEBBIE HAS SOME
NICE COLD ICE TEA FOR HIM. (Almost
as cold as her heart)

MIKE GOES HOME AND WASHES
UP AND THEN CALLS DEBBIE TO SEE
IF SHE'D LIKE TO GO TO THE RACES
TONIGHT.

SHE TELLS HIM SHE IS TOO TIRED
TO GO ANYWHERE.

SO HE ASKS IF HE CAN COME
OVER AND KEEP HER COMPANY,
NO!!!!
YOU SEE SHE DOESN'T NEED MIKE
ANYMORE AND SHE GOES TO WORK
AND ASKS HER FRIEND SUE WHAT
SHE CAN DO TO GET RID OF MIKE.
SUE TELLS HER IT MIGHT HAVE
BEEN EASIER IF SHE WOULDN'T
HAVE TAKEN HIM TO BED. (my my)
SUE SAYS THE BEST WAY TO GET
RID OF MIKE IS TO TELL HIM YOUR
OLD HUSBAND IS BACK AND YOU
DECIDED TO GET BACK TOGETHER.
(In other words lie)
NOW YOU HAVE A GIRL YOU LIKE,
BUT SHE'S GOING OUT WITH ONE OF
YOUR FRIENDS, AND SHE KNOWS
YOU LIKE HER.

YOU'RE A NICE GUY AND WON'T MAKE A MOVE ON HER BECAUSE OF YOUR FRIEND. (And we all know what happens to nice guys. right)!!!

WELL GUESS WHAT HAPPENS. YOUR FRIEND BREAKS UP WITH HER AND DOESN'T WANT TO SEE HER AGAIN. NOW THIS FRIEND OF YOURS IS THROWING A PARTY TOMORROW AT HIS HOUSE. HIS OLD GIRLFRIEND WAS GOING TO BE THERE WITH HIM BUT NOT NOW. (She knows you like her) WHAT TO DO .. WELL, SHE'S ABOUT TO DO IT TO YOU. HAVING KNOWLEDGE OF YOUR INTEREST IN HER AND KNOWING YOU'LL BE GOING TO THE PARTY. SHE SAYS TO YOU "I KNOW HOW YOU FEEL ABOUT ME AND SINCE

YOUR FRIEND BROKE UP WITH ME, I THOUGHT WE COULD GO TO THE PARTY TOGETHER".

WOW, SHE KNOWS HOW YOU FEEL.

YOU THINK "OH BOY", I HAVE A CHANCE!!!!

SHE'S USING YOU TO GET INTO THE PARTY TO TRY AND GET HER BOYFRIEND BACK (sorry)!!!

YOU AND HER AREN'T AT THE PARTY MORE THAN TWO MINUTES AND YOU DON'T KNOW WHAT HAPPEN TO YOUR DATE.

YOU DON'T WANT HER TO FEEL YOUR POSSESSIVE. SO YOU DON'T GO CHASING AFTER HER!! AFTER SITTING BY YOURSELF FOR ABOUT 20 MINUTES YOU THINK {Lets see where she's at}..!! (My, my, my) THERE SHE IS, KISSING HER OLD BOYFRIEND. EVEN THOUGH SHE KNEW YOU HAD FEELINGS FOR HER AND SO DO MOST PEOPLE {"WHO ARE YOUR FRIENDS NOT HERS"} AND THEY ALL SEE WHAT'S HAPPENING. YOU FEEL LIKE A DUMB FOOL. (Kathy'S clown) YOU LEAVE WITH YOUR TAIL BETWEEN YOUR LEGS.

ALWAYS REMEMBER A WOMAN ONLY CARES ABOUT HER OWN FEELINGS NOT YOURS!!!! IF A WOMAN KNOWS YOUR FEELINGS SHE'LL USE THEM AGAINST YOU EVERY TIME!!!!

WHEN YOU LET THEM KNOW YOU LOVE THEM, WATCH OUT BECAUSE EVERY TIME YOU DON'T DO WHAT

SHE WANTS. THE FIRST THING OUT OF HER MOUTH IS WELL, "I'M GOING TO LEAVE YOU". NOW YOU'LL DO ANYTHING.

JUST DON'T LEAVE ME PLEASEEEEEEEEEE. (My.. my.. my) "GET HOLD OF YOURSELF. NEVER BEG A WOMAN, BECAUSE BEGGARS DON'T HAVE MONEY. SHE'S NOT HEARING A WORD YOUR SAYING, NOW A NEW WATCH MAYBE.

CHAPTER TWO

SEX AND ORGASM PLEASE

DON'T LET PEOPLE UNDER 18 YEARS OLD READ THIS CHAPTER" RATED "R" LETS SAY YOU HAVE A WOMAN WHO SAYS SHE LOVES YOU. YOU HAVE A GOOD JOB. YOU GIVE HER WHATEVER SHE NEEDS. UNBEKNOWNST TO YOU SHE'S NOT SATISFIED IN BED BUT DOESN'T TELL YOU. YOU DON'T KNOW BECAUSE SHE SCREAMS TO HIGH HEAVEN WHEN YOU MAKE LOVE TO HER. (She fakes, it) WHEN YOU GO TO WORK SHE HAS SOME BUM COME OVER (WHO DOESN'T HAVE A JOB OR MONEY)!!!!

WHAT HE DOES HAVE IS A SEX DRIVE THAT MAKES HIM SCREW YOUR GIRL FOR TWO HOURS AND DOES SHE SCREAM NOW. (oh yea). SHE STAYS WITH YOU, BECAUSE YOU TAKE CARE OF HER AND PAY THE BILLS.

SHE FEELS AS LONG AS YOU DON'T KNOW ABOUT HER BUM…NO HARM DONE. THAT'S THE MIND OF WOMEN!!!!

ALL WOMEN HAVE A NAUGHTY SIDE TO THEM THAT THEY ONLY SHOW TO STRANGERS SO THEIR NOT EMBARRASSED BY THEM.

THIS IS THE SIDE WHERE SHE GIVES INTO HER UNINHIBITED SIDE OF SEX, ONLY GOING WITH THE

STRONG DESIRE SHE FEELS, IT'S THE TOTAL DIRTY SIDE OF LUST!!!! MAYBE SHE'S 36 YEARS OLD AND THE PAPER BOY AT 17 LOOKS PRETTY TASTY AND HER MAN ISN'T HOME AT THE TIME. JUST THINK WHAT SHE COULD DO WITH THAT YOUNG MEAT. AND YOU KNOW HOW YOU WOULD HAVE LIKED THAT WHEN YOU WERE THAT AGE. OH BOY!!

SO IF YOU START GETTING HOME DELIVERY AND DIDN'T ORDER IT LOOK OUT.

THIS IS THE SIDE WHERE SHE WANTS TWO PENISES RATHER THAN ONE ORWANTS TO BE WITH ANOTHER WOMAN. MAYBE JUST BY HERSELF WITH HER ELECTRIC

DEVICES. SOME MIGHT WANT SOME
BACK DOOR TREATMENT OR WHAT
EVER HER IMAGINATION CAN COME
UP WITH.

MAYBE SHE LIKES SPANKED AND
THINKS YOU WILL LOOK AT HER
FUNNY. THAT'S WHY A STRANGER IS
BETTER SO THE STORIES WON'T GET
AROUND AND SHE CAN STILL ACT
LIKE A PURE INNOCENT CLEAN CUT
WOMAN.

SO IF YOU WANT SOME TRUE WILD
SEX THAT YOUR WOMAN IS HOLDING
OUT ON YOU.

TALK TO HER LET HER KNOW
THAT YOU JUST WANT TO PLEASE
HER. IN ANY MANNER SHE WANTS
JUST OPEN UP TO YOU SO YOU CAN

**BOTH ENJOY THE HIDDEN LUST
THAT ALL WOMEN HAVE!!!!
BECAUSE WOMEN NO LONGER
HAVE ANY MORALS.
THIS IS ONE OF THE LEADING
REASONS WHY THIS COUNTRY IS
GOING TO HELL.
WOMEN USED TO BE THE KEEPERS
OF MORALS BY SAYING NO TO MEN
AND PROTECTING HERSELF TO STAY
A VIRGIN!!!!
NOW THEY SAY "WHY CAN'T WE
BE AS IMMORAL AS MEN!!!!
THAT'S WHY ABORTION IS LEGAL.
SO WOMEN CAN HAVE ALL THE SEX
THEY WANT, WITHOUT FACING ANY
RESPONSIBILITY.
SO NOW THERE ARE NO MORALS!!!**

REMEMBER MEN ONLY HAVE THAT DRIVE FOR SEX,.. WHILE WOMEN WERE SUPPOSED TO BE HARD TO GET!

THEY CARE MORE ABOUT SEX THEN THEY CARE ABOUT MOTHERHOOD.

IN ALL THE ANIMAL KINGDOM, THE FEMALE WILL DIE BEFORE SHE'LL LET HARM COME TO HER BABY.

JUST KNOWING THAT THIS GOES AGAINST NATURE, AND THE WORD OF GOD, SHOULD TELL YOU THAT THIS IS IMMORAL. TO A WOMAN, A BABY IS NO MORE THAN AN INCONVENIENCE!!!!

BUT SO WHAT!!!! SHE JUST WANTS HER CLIMAX!!!!

WHO CARES ABOUT MORALS SURELY NOT WOMEN. WHEN THE SHIP IS SINKING THEY YELL "WOMEN AND CHILDREN FIRST." SO A WOMEN SAYS "SEE WOMEN ARE EVEN BEFORE CHILDREN." A WOMAN WILL GO TO BED WITH TWO MEN, OR THREE MEN, TWO MEN AND ANOTHER WOMAN, WITH A DOG WITH, A MACHINE VIBRATOR, A HORSE, A WASHING MACHINE OR ANYTHING ELSE IF SHE THINKS IT WILL JUST GIVE HER AN ORGASM. YES, THIS IS TRUE, BUT A WOMAN WON'T TELL YOU THIS BECAUSE SHE WANTS TO PORTRAY HERSELF AS MORAL AND RESPECTABLE.

SO SOME OTHER GUY OR WOMAN IS GETTING YOUR UNINHIBITED SEX FROM YOUR WOMAN.

SHE'LL NEVER TELL YOU UNTIL YOUR KID NEEDS A BODY PART AND YOUR NOT A MATCH.!!!!!!! (imagine that)

THE KID THAT'S 14 YEARS OLD THAT YOU HAVE BEEN FEEDING, CLOTHING, AND HOUSING IS NOT EVEN YOUR SON. ((surprise .surprise)

THE WHOLE PROBLEM IS MEN ARE STILL LOOKING AT WOMEN LIKE THEIR MOTHER, BECAUSE THEIR MOTHER WAS BROUGHT UP DECENT. BUT NOW YOU HAVE TO REALIZE YOUR MOTHER ISN'T RAISING THEM NOW.

THERE ARE SOME THINGS YOUR WIFE OR GIRLFRIEND IS TELLING YOUR YOUNG DAUGHTER BUT NOT TELLING YOU.

YOU KNOW IT'S "OK" NOT TO BE A VIRGIN ANYMORE. IT'S "OK" TO HAVE MORE THAN ONE BOYFRIEND AND IT'S "OK" TO BE DECEITFUL. LETS GET YOU SOME BIRTH CONTROL PILLS. YOU KNOW WE DON'T WANT ANY SURPRISES POPPING UP LATER AND DON'T WORRY YOUR FATHER DOESN'T NEED TO KNOW.

JUST ASK YOUR WOMAN WHO MADE SURE YOUR DAUGHTER GOT THE PILL. YOU KNOW ITS "OK" FOR HER TO DATE MORE THEN ONE BOY AT A TIME.

JUST ASK YOUR WOMAN AND SHE'LL TELL YOU IT WILL KEEP THEM FROM GETTING TOO SERIOUS. WELL MY GOD, WHY IN THE WORLD WOULD I WANT MY DAUGHTER TO BE SERIOUS ABOUT A RELATIONSHIP?

YOUR WOMAN WILL TELL HER, YOU SHOULD HAVE ALL THE FUN YOU WANT. YOU KNOW BECAUSE MEN DO. I THOUGHT THAT'S WHAT WAS WRONG, NO MORALS. NO ITS ONLY WRONG TO WOMEN, IF THEY CAN'T PARTICIPATE IN IT!!!

SO MEN WATCH YOUR DAUGHTERS, I GUARANTEE THAT YOUR WOMAN IS TEACHING HER TO BE DECEITFUL EVEN TO YOU, HER OWN FATHER.

NOW ONE NIGHT I'M AT A BAR
WITH A FRIEND WHERE DRINKING
BEER AND PLAYING THE SIX CARD
MACHINE.
ALL OF A SUDDEN THIS WOMAN
RUSHES UP TO US AND SAYS, HURRY
UP THE CAR IS STILL RUNNING!!
I ASKED WHAT THE HELL DOES
YOUR CAR HAVE TO DO WITH ME??
SHE LOOKS AT ME AND SAYS I
NEED SEX I'M A NYMPHO AND I
WANT YOU TWO TO COME WITH ME.
I SAY LOOK I JUST BOUGHT A
BEER WAIT TILL I'M DONE WITH IT.
JEFF STARTS TO LAUGH.
SHE SAYS LOOK I'M NOT FOOLING
I NEED SEX NOW HERE'S $20.oo NOW
COME ON LET'S GO.

AS JEFF AND I ARE LEAVING WE
SEE BOBBY COMING IN AND HE SAYS
SHE'S CRAZY SHE WOULDN'T LET ME
COME BACK TILL I TOLD HER
WHERE SHE COULD FIND SOME
MORE MEN!!! (OH MY)
AS WE DRIVE TO HER HOUSE SHE
SAYS THAT HER HUSBAND IS OUT OF
TOWN ON A BUSINESS TRIP HE
WORKS FOR A PHONE COMPANY,
THAT HER HUSBAND AND HER HAVE
ORGIES ALL THE TIME AND HE
KNOWS HER NEEDS SO SHE ISN'T
DOING ANYTHING WRONG!! (WELL
ALL RIGHT)!!!
WHEN WE GOT TO HER HOUSE SHE
SAYS DOES ANY ONE WANT TO TAKE
A SHOWER AND JEFF SAYS YES.

SHE TELLS ME TO WAIT ON THE
BED AND CHECK OUT WHAT'S IN THE
DRAWER SEE IF YOU FIND
SOMETHING YOU LIKE??
WILL NOW I GOT TO LOOK,!!
AND O 'MY SHE HAS ALL KINDS OF
ELECTRICAL DEVICES IN THE
DRAWER WITH EXTRA BATTERIES.
THIS WOMAN IS DEFINITELY INTO
SOME HEAVY SEX, OF ANY KIND.
NOW SHE COMES OVER TO ME
AND SAYS HERE TAKE THIS SMALL
ONE. COME ON NOW THIS THING IS
ONLY AS BIG AS MY SMALL FINGER,
WHAT COULD YOU DO WITH THIS
AND LET ME TELL YOU SHE SHOWED
ME!!! (I'M NOT TELLING YOU)
WE MOVE DOWNSTAIRS AND ARE
ON THE FLOOR WHEN I SEE TWO

LITTLE FEET AND I LOOK BACK AND
HERE'S A LITTLE GIRL
THE LITTLE GIRL SAYS MOTHER
CAN I JOIN IN (WHAT!!!!!!!)
THE MOTHER TELLS THE LITTLE
GIRL, NOT TONIGHT HONEY THESE
MEN ARE FOR MOMMY!!!
I'M OUT THE DOOR NO RIDE BACK
NO GOOD-BY EXCEPT TO SAY HOW
SICK THIS WOMAN WAS. WHAT
MOTHER WOULD EXPOSE THEIR
CHILD TO SOMETHING LIKE THIS. (I
FOR ONE DON'T KNOW), AND TILL
THIS DAY 30 YEARS LATER I STILL
DON'T KNOW. (YES I DID REPORT
HER AND HER HUSBAND TO THE
POLICE)
WHEN HER HUSBAND GOT BACK
FROM HIS TRIP HE WENT ON

ANOTHER ONE AND DIDN'T NEED AN AIRLINE TICKET.

THESE ARE THINGS THAT MADE ME AWARE THAT YOU NEVER KNOW WHAT YOU MIGHT GET YOURSELF INVOLVED WITH BY LEAVING WITH A WOMAN THAT'S MOTORS RUNNING. (TURN IT OFF CHECK IT OUT FIRST AND LISTEN TO YOUR FRIEND WHEN HE TELLS YOU SHE CRAZY).

OH WHAT HAPPEN TO JEFF, WILL JEFF STOPPED GOING TO BARS ALTOGETHER.

MY ONE FRIEND HAD A YOUNG GIRLFRIEND AND SHE CAME OVER TO MY PLACE IN THE MIDDLE OF THE NIGHT.

I WAS SLEEPING IN THE BACK OF
MY STORE AT THE TIME TRYING TO
STOP BREAK IN'S.

SO AT THREE O'CLOCK IN THE
MORNING THIS LITTLE BLONDE HAIR
GIRL JUST SHORT OF THE AGE OF 18
IS HERE TO ASK ME TO HELP HER
GET INTO PETER HOUSE!!

WELL HE'S MAD AT ME SHE SAYS,
AND IT'S HIS BIRTHDAY (WE HAD A
FIGHT). SO YOU HAD A FIGHT WITH
PETER WHAT WAS IT ABOUT?

SHE TELLS ME THAT SHE HAD
GOTTEN PETER THREE GOOD
LOOKING GIRLS TO GO TO BED WITH
HIM AT THE SAME TIME FOR HIS
BIRTHDAY PRESENT.

YOUR TELLING ME HE'S MAD AT
YOU BECAUSE OF THIS, WHAT

WHERE YOU STANDING IN THE ROOM WHEN HE WAS SUPPOSE TO GET BUSY.

SHE SAID NO THAT SHE HAD WENT INTO ANOTHER ROOM WITH THREE GUYS. AND PETER JUST GOT UP AND LEFT.

SO YOU DIDN'T GO HOME WITH HIM. NO I STAYED AND WHEN I GOT HOME HE HAD LOCKED ME OUT.

PATTY YOU DIDN'T GET PETER A PRESENT YOU GOT YOUR SELF A PRESENT. PETER LEFT BECAUSE HE LOVES YOU AND DIDN'T WANT OTHER WOMEN.

BUT YOU STAYED AND HAD ALL THE SEX YOU COULD GET NOT CARING OF HOW YOU MADE HIM FEEL.

**YOU GOT HIM THE GIRLS SO YOU
COULD SAY THAT HE HAD THE SAME
CHANCE AS YOU.**

**I TOLD HER I WOULD TAKE HER
OVER BUT I HOPED THAT PETER
WOULDN'T LET HER IN BUT HE DID.**

**A MAN DOESN'T KNOW HOW TO
THINK WHEN HE'S IN LOVE, NONE OF
US DO, WE HIDE FROM IT SO MUCH
THAT WHEN IT SHOWS UP WE'RE
LOST ON HOW TO HANDLE IT. (SAD
BUT TRUE).**

**THEN THERE'S THIS STRANGE
THING ABOUT WOMEN ALSO.**

**I USED TO BE WELL KNOWN FOR
MOUNTAIN PARTY'S THAT I HELD
EVERY SPRING.**

THE NUMBERS WHERE 2 TO 1
THAT'S RIGHT TWO GIRLS FOR EACH
MALE THAT WOULD COME.

THE GUYS ALL HAD TO PAY $10.00
EACH. THE GIRLS WHERE LET IN FOR
FREE!! (OF COURSE) YOU SEE THE
FIRST THING YOU SHOULD KNOW
THAT BACK IN 1969 THAT 45% OF THE
GIRLS AREN'T GOING TO GIVE UP
ANY SEX.

NOW THE WHOLE IDEA OF THE
MOUNTAIN PARTY IS TO GET THE
GIRLS IN THE WOODS AWAY FROM
THE HOME AND GETTING THEM TO
SPEND THE NIGHT.

(YOU HAVE A BETTER CHANCE TO
HAVE SEX IF THE GIRLS ARE IN ON
THE AGREEMENT.)

TURNING OFF THE MAIN ROAD
ONTO THE SMALL DIRT AND ROCKY
ROAD FOR ABOUT 700 YARDS FROM
THE ENTRANCE TO PARADISE. NOW
IT OPEN UP TO A LARGE OPEN
MEADOW WITH A LOWER LEDGE
RUNNING ALONG THE SMALL
STREAM.

THE LOWER LEDGE WAS USED
FOR COUPLES AT NIGHT, YOU SEE.,
YOU COULDN'T SEE DOWN THERE AT
NIGHT, BECAUSE OF A LONG
SHADOW THAT WOULD COME FROM
THE UPPER FIELD WHERE THE TWO
KEGS OF BEER WAS BURIED IN THE
GROUND PATCH IN ICE, ALONG WITH
THE GENERATOR THAT POWER THE
AMP TO PLAY THE MUSIC OVER 6
BOSE 901 SPEAKERS!!

NOTHING LIKE LISTENING TO HENDIX IN THE MOUNTAINS.

OK NOW WITH ALL THE CARS PARK DOWN IN THE FIELD WITH US, SO NO ONE EVER KNEW THAT THERE WAS A PARTY GOING ON. THE ONLY TWO RULES, WHERE NO FIGHTING AND NO ONE COULD LEAVE UNTIL THE NEXT DAY, SO NO ONE WOULD BE DRUNK WHILE DRIVING TWO SMALL RULES, BUT IT KEPT THE PARTY FUN AND SAFE (WE DIDN'T NEED A LAW FOR WHAT COMMON SINCE TOLD YOU!).

THAT'S ONE THING WOMAN WANT AND THAT'S TO KNOW THERE SAFE. HAVING ENOUGH GIRLS ALWAYS HELP KEEP FIGHTS FROM HAPPENING.

SLOWLY AS THE SUNSTARTED TO
SET AND THE AIR STARTING TO GET
COOLER.

THE PARTY GOERS WOULD START
PAIRING OFF!!

THERE WHERE COUPLES IN CARS,
DOWN ON THE LEDGE, BACK IN THE
WOODS, AND THE ONE'S THAT DON'T
DO THE NASTY ARE ALL HANGING
AROUND THE FIRE, LAUGHING
ABOUT WHAT THE OTHERS ARE
DOING. (MY MY).

THIS IS ONE OF THE REASON THIS
PARTY WAS IN THE SPRING WITH
TEMP DOWN GIRL LIKE TO CUDDLE
IN THE COLD AND AFTER YOUR IN
THE WOODS ALONE FOR ABOUT 20
MIN.'S THE GIRL AND YOU WOULD

**JUMP UP AND RUN LIKE HELL TO
GET BACK BY THE FIRE.
THERE WAS NO TALKING AND YOU
COULD BE ON THE OTHER SIDE OF
THE FIRE CHECKING OUT ANOTHER
GIRL AND MIGHT NOT KNOW THE
LAST ONES NAME .(Bad Boy).
WE ALWAYS HAD GOOD FOOD
WITH THE MONEY WE COULD GET
THE KEGS FOR ABOUT $18.00 EACH
AND CHICKEN DIDN'T COST MUCH
BACK IN THE 60'S ABOUT .29 CENTS A
LBS. SO YOU COULD GET ABOUT 120
DRUM STICKS FOR ABOUT $9.00 THE
SHRIMP COST ABOUT $20.00 FOR 50
LBS. WHAT EVER WAS LEFT WENT
FOR HARD LIQUOR.**

TOTAL COST OF PARTY WAS
USUALLY ABOUT $150.00 SO THAT'S
WHAT WE HAD 15GUYS TO 30 GIRLS.
NOW THE GUYS THAT CAME
WHERE BUILD LIKE WASH BROADS
AND CUTE THEY ALL HAD MANNERS,
BUT BASICALLY AS MY WIFE WOULD
SAY THERE PIGS!!! (THANK YOU
VERY MUCH).
THIS IS WHY THE GIRL WOULD
COME PLUS THEY LIKED THE
SHRIMP. MUSIC AND SPOOKINESS OF
IT.
GIRLS LIKE SPOOKY, WE USED TO
TAKE GIRLS TO A PLACE CALLED
MUMMY'S HILL AN OLD CEMETERY
THAT WAS ON THE SIDE OF THE
MOUNTAIN.

THERE WOULD BE OPEN GRAVES ONCE IN A WHILE. PEOPLE WHERE MOVING THERE RELATIVES TO A DIFFERENT CEMETERY.

WE WOULD TAKE ONE GUY UP THERE EARLY AND HE WOULD GET INTO ONE OF THE OPEN GRAVES SO WHEN WE CAME BACK WITH THE GIRLS HE COULD JUMP OUT TO SCARE ALL THE GIRLS!!! THEY WOULD START SCARING AND RUNNING AND SOME TIMES THEY PEE THEMSELVES.

BUT LATER THEY ALWAYS GOT CLOSE TO YOU. (NAUGHTY GIRL.) SORRY ABOUT THAT I JUST THOUGHT OF THAT WHILE I WAS WRITING THIS.

LETS GET BACK TO THE
MOUNTAIN.
THERE WAS ONE LARGE TENT FOR
ANYONE TOO SLEEP IN IF THEY
DIDN'T WANT TO SLEEP UNDER THE
STARS SOME MORNINGS WHEN I
WOULD GO TO WAKE EVERYONE UP
THEY WERE STACK TWO HIGH IN
THE TENT, BUT THEY WHERE WARM.
(Don't pass Gas Please).
I GOT THE SAME QUESTION EACH
PARTY AROUND 10 O-CLOCK P.M.
WHERE DO WE GO TO THE
BATHROOM?
NOW THESE GIRLS ASKING THE
QUESTION HAVE ALREADY BEEN IN
THE WOODS WITH A GUY OR TWO!
AND I WOULD SAY THAT TO THEM,
WHAT ARE YOU TALKING ABOUT

YOU JUST USED THE WOODS YOU WHERE JUST OUT THERE WITH YOUR PANTS DOWN SO WHAT WAS THE BIG DEAL. (GEEEEEEEEEeE)!!!!

FOR SOME REASON THE WOMAN OR GIRL CAN DO ANYTHING IN THE WOODS BUT PEE?

THERE ARE WOMEN OUT THERE THAT THINK THEY ARE SO HOT AND GOOD LOOKING THAT NO MAN WILL TURN THEM DOWN.

WELL I TURN WOMEN LIKE THIS DOWN EVERY TIME.

JUST TO LET THEM KNOW THEY AREN'T THAT SPECIAL AT ALL!!

SOME OF THESE WOMEN HAVEN'T HAD THIS EVER HAPPEN TO THEM BEFORE, Soooo.

**THEY HAVE TO GET BACK AT YOU
FOR TURNING THEM DOWN!!
ONE OF THESE TYPES OF WOMEN
TOLD SOME FRIENDS OF MINE THAT I
WAS MESSING AROUND WITH THEIR
WIVES.
NOW THESE FRIENDS OF MINE
COME TO SEE ME AND WANT TO
FIGHT. (uh ho)
I WOULDN'T FIGHT MY FRIENDS
BECAUSE I KNEW THIS WOMAN HAD
DONE AND I WONT FIGHT OVER
LIES!!!!
I LOST TWO OF THESE FRIENDS
AND ONE OF THEM HAD GOTTEN A
DIVORCED, BECAUSE OF THESE LIES.
THIS GUY LEFT HIS WOMAN
NEVER BELIEVING HER OR ME THAT
THIS HAD NEVER HAPPENED.**

HE SAID WHAT REASON WOULD
THIS WOMAN MAKE UP SUCH A
STORY LIKE THIS IF IT WASN'T TRUE.
NOT CARING HOW HER LIES HAD
AFFECTED OTHER PEOPLE LIVES.
ONLY WANTING TO GET EVEN FOR
BEING SPURNED!!!!
THIS IS ONE OF THE WORST TYPES
OF WOMEN AND VERY DANGEROUS.
DANGEROUS BECAUSE, THIS TYPE IS
SO GOOD LOOKING AND BUILT SO
WELL THAT MEN ARE BLINDED TO
THE TRUE UGLINESS OR EVIL OF
THIS INDIVIDUAL!!!!
THERE ARE OTHER SICK WOMEN
OUT THERE LIKE THE ONE THE FIRE
DEPARTMENT HAD TO BE CALLED BY
THE POLICE WHO WHERE PASSING
THE BUCK BECAUSE THEY DIDN'T

WANT TO GET INVOLVED WITH THE WOMAN THAT NEEDED HELP?

LETS ME START AT THE BEGINNING. THE CAB OFFICE WAS CALLED BY THE WOMAN SAYING SHE NEEDED HELP. A CAB WAS DISPATCHED, I WAS THE DRIVER.

WHEN I ARRIVED AT THE ADDRESS I WAS TOLD TO GO TO THE DOOR AND KNOCK. THE WOMAN INSIDE SAID COME IN HURRY.

WHEN I WALKED IN THE DOOR, WHAT I SAW, I WAS NOT PREPARED FOR.

HERE WAS A WOMAN NAKED ON THE FLOOR ON ALL FOURS WITH A GREAT DANE MOUNTED ON HER BACK. (she was locked up) I DIDN'T KNOW HOW TO GET A 180 LB. DOG

OFF A WOMAN, AND I DIDN'T WANT
TO GET BITE. SO I TOLD HER I
WOULD CALL THE POLICE THINKING
THEY WOULD BE ABLE TO DO
SOMETHING.

INSTEAD WHEN THE POLICE
ARRIVED THEY DECIDED TO CALL IN
THE FIRE DEPARTMENT!!!

I ASKED THE POLICE WHY WOULD
YOU CALL THE FIRE DEPARTMENT
AND THEY SAID WHENEVER THEY
WANT TO BREAK UP DOGS DOING
THE SAME THING THEY ALWAYS
THREW COLD WATER ON THEM. (Ha
Ha).

WELL FOR THOSE WHO DON'T
KNOW WHAT LOCKED UP IS. YOU SEE
SOMETIMES THE MALE DOGS
PENISES WILL SWELL UP IN A HARD

KNOT AND CAN'T GET LOOSE FROM THEIR PARTNERS!!!!

(EVIDENTLY THIS WOMAN DIDN'T KNOW THIS).

A WOMAN NOT KNOWING THIS IS SOME WHAT EMBARRASSED WHEN FOUND OUT. (my my the dirty dog)

SO MY ADVICE IS GO OUT WITH A MEXICAN GIRL THEY ONLY HAVE CHIHUAHUA!!! (Always wear a rubber).

ANOTHER RULE I GO BY IS TO BE AS UNFRIENDLY A PERSON AS I CAN TO MY FRIENDS WIVES.

YOU SEE WHEN A WOMAN GETS MAD AT THEIR MATE SOMETIMES THEY LIKE TO HIT ON THEIR HUSBAND'S BEST FRIEND IN ORDER TO HURT THEM MORE.

NOW I HAVE A FRIEND WHO LIKED TO DRINK TOO MUCH SO HIS WIFE ASKED ME TO GO TO THE BAR AND PICK HIM UP BECAUSE HE COULDN'T DRIVE HOME.

WHEN I GOT HIM TO HIS HOUSE I ASKED HIS WIFE WHERE I SHOULD DROP HIM. SHE SAID TO TAKE HIM UPSTAIRS AND PUT HIM ON THE BED. SO I DID.

AS I WAS TRYING TO LEAVE SHE STOPPED ME SAYING SHE NEEDED TO TALK. (Oh my, I was thinking.)

SHE SAID "WOULD YOU LIKE SOME COFFEE", (AT THREE IN THE MORNING) I SAID "O. K.)" SHE STARTS TO TELL ME HOW SHE LOVES HER HUSBAND, BUT THOUGHT THAT

ONCE THEY GOT MARRIED, THAT HE
WOULD CHANGE.

OH BOY, HOW MANY TIMES HAVE I
HEARD THIS. I COULD NEVER
UNDERSTAND WHY WOMEN ALWAYS
WANT A MAN TO CHANGE. WHY
DON'T THEY FIND THE GUY WITH
THE QUALITIES THAT THEY WANT
TO START WITH.

WELL THAT'S BECAUSE THOSE
QUALITIES ARE BORING, AND
BEFORE THEY WANTED THAT WILD
MUSTANG. NOT THE BORING GUY
THEY NEVER GONE OUT WITH.

I TOLD HER THAT SHE KNEW
WHAT HE WAS LIKE BEFORE SHE
MARRIED HIM. HE WAS A DRUNK AND
LIKED TO PARTY ALL NIGHT LONG
AND THAT WAS WHAT SHE LIKE

ABOUT HIM. (But now that their married
it's not what she wants).

NOW WHY CAN'T A WOMAN EVER
FIND THE ONE SHE WANTS BEFORE
THEY GET MARRIED. SO HE WOULD
ALREADY BE THE WAY SHE WANTS
HIM.

ANYHOW I TELL HER THAT IF SHE
WANTS TO SEE SOME KIND OF
CHANGE. THEN SHE WOULD HAVE TO
DO SOMETHING.

LOOK I SAY YOU HAVE BEEN
MARRIED ABOUT THREE TEARS NOW
AND YOU DON'T HAVE ANY
CHILDREN. I TELL HER THAT YOU
WOULD BE SURPRISED HOW A CHILD
MAKES A MAN MORE RESPONSIBLE.

SHE JUMPS UP AND YELLS, OH
YEAH AND TIE MYSELF DOWN!!

HEARING HER MAKE A STATEMENT LIKE THIS I KNEW THIS WOMAN WAS GOING TO DUMP MY FRIEND. (my my) I MEAN WHY ELSE WOULDN'T SHE WANT A CHILD.

YOU SEE SHE WAS LIKE HER HUSBAND, SHE LIKED TO PARTY TOO. I MADE IT A POINT TO RUN INTO MY FRIEND THE NEXT DAY.

WHEN I SAW HIM I ASKED HIM IF HE AND HIS WIFE HAD A JOINT ACCOUNTS?

HE SAYS YES THEY DID. I SAID GET YOUR MONEY OUT BECAUSE YOUR WIFE IS GETTING READY TO LEAVE YOU. HE SAYS NO WAY.

YOUR NUTS! That's why they never see what is in front of them) YOU KNOW

MOST PEOPLE WILL NEVER BELIEVE
THINGS ABOUT THEIR MATES.

I'M NOT ONE TO SAY SOMETHING
BECAUSE I ALREADY KNOW THIS,
BUT I WANT TO MAKE SURE THAT
THIS WOMAN DOESN'T GET THE
JUMP ON A FRIEND.

BUT YOU SEE I NEVER REPEAT A
WARNING IF YOU DON'T TAKE IT THE
FIRST TIME,. THEN I HAVE NO PITY
FOR YOU.

EIGHT DAYS GO BY AND HIS WIFE
ASKED ME IF I WOULD TAKE HER
HUSBAND OUT SO SHE COULD HAVE
A SURPRISE BIRTHDAY PARTY FOR
HIM!!

SO I DID THIS AND I'M THINKING
THAT THIS WON'T BE MUCH OF A
SURPRISE ONCE WE GET BACK

BECAUSE ALL THE CARS WOULD BE
THERE WHEN WE WOULD GET BACK.
AS WE WERE DRIVING BACK TO
THE HOUSE HE SAW ALL THE CARS
AND STARTS LAUGHING AND SAID
DON'T WORRY I'LL ACT SURPRISED.
NOW WE'RE BACK AT THE HOUSE
AND AFTER ABOUT AN HOUR MY
FRIEND COMES OVER AND TAKES ME
ASIDE.
HE SAYS TO ME IF SHE WAS GOING
TO LEAVE HIM WHY WAS SHE
THROWING THIS PARTY FOR HIM!!
TOLD HIM TO THINK OF IT AS A
GOING AWAY PARTY AND ASKED HIM
IF HE GOT HIS MONEY OUT OF THE
BANK YET?

HE SAID "COLEMAN YOU JUST DON'T TRUST WOMEN!!! (Duuhhh no shit!!!).

SO NOW ABOUT TWO DAYS LATER I GET A PHONE CALL FROM MY FRIEND AND HE'S YELLING AND CRYING AT THE SAME TIME TRYING TO TELL ME WHAT'S HAPPENING. HERE'S WHAT HE SAYS. HE CAME HOME EARLY BECAUSE HE WAS HURT AT WORK AND AS HE WAS GOING DOWN THE STREET HIS WIFE WAS GOING UP THE STREET AND NOT ALONE!!!

THERE WAS A LARGE BLOND MALE DRIVING A TRUCK WITH ALL MY FRIENDS FURNITURE AND HIS WIFE IN IT. (my my) HE TURNED AROUND AND FOLLOWED THEM TO

**AN APARTMENT COMPLEX THAT
TAKES ABOUT TWO TO THREE
MONTHS TO GET INTO!!!
SHE'S MOVING THE FURNITURE IN
AND SO IS THE BLONDE HAIR GUY!!!
I ASKED HIM ABOUT THE MONEY
IN THE BANK AND HE SAYS IT'S ALL
GONE!!!
HE COULDN'T BELIEVE THIS WAS
HAPPENING TO HIM!!!
HE MUST OF THOUGHT HIS WIFE
LOVED HIM, HUH!!!!
NOW LETS THINK ABOUT THIS.
THIS WOMAN HAD PLANNED THIS
MONTHS AHEAD OF TIME AND THIS
BLONDE WAS NOT SOMEONE SHE
HAD JUST MET YESTERDAY.**

SHE HAD A RELATIONSHIP WITH THIS BLONDE GOING ON FOR A FEW MONTHS.

SO SHE WAS SLEEPING WITH HER HUSBAND AND HAVING SEX WITH HIM AND ALL THE TIME SHE HAD THIS GUY ON THE SIDE!!!!

SHE MADE YOU THINK SHE STILL LOVED YOU!!!

NOW HOW DO YOU HAVE SEX WITH SOMEONE YOU NO LONGER LOVE.

SHE'S HAVING SEX WITH HER HUSBAND AND TELLING HIM THERE IS NO ONE ELSE.

SHE ALSO IS HAVING SEX WITH HER NEW PLAYMATE AND TELLING HIM SHE NO LONGER HAS SEX WITH HER OLD MAN.

Ronald Jessy Coleman

SO SHE LIED TO HER EX. AND TO
HER NEW BOYFRIEND AT THE SAME
TIME AND NEVER BATTED AN EYE
LID.
OH BY THE WAY HAPPY BIRTHDAY
STEVE!!!!
NOW THIS SHOULD SHOW YOU
HOW DECEITFUL AND SNEAKY A
WOMAN CAN BE AND LOOK AS IF SHE
WAS AN ANGEL ALL THE TIME.
WERE YOU EVER MARRIED TO A
WOMAN WHO CALLS HER PARENTS
TO SETTLE THE FIGHTS YOU'RE
HAVING OVER MONEY.
DOES THIS MAKE SENSE TO YOU?
THESE ARE THE SAME PEOPLE
THAT TAUGHT HER IT'S OK TO DO
WHAT EVER SHE WANTS!!! YOU
KNOW IF YOU NEED MORE MONEY

YOUR HUSBAND CAN JUST GET ANOTHER JOB.

RIGHT!!!!

HER FATHER WANTS TO KNOW WHY YOUR NOT TAKING BETTER CARE OF HIS LITTLE (SPOILED BRAT) GIRL.

HER MOTHER WANTS TO KNOW WHY YOU CAN'T HELP HER DAUGHTER MORE WITH THE HOUSE WORK.

YOUR WIFE IS SCREAMING AT YOU TO LISTEN TO HER FATHERS ADVICE!!!! WELL HERE'S SOME ADVICE FOR HER PARENTS!!!

THE NEXT LITTLE GIRL YOU RAISE. TEACH HER TO THINK FOR HERSELF CAUSE HER HUSBAND ONLY MARRIED HER.

NOT THE TWO OF YOU.
TEACH HER TO ADD SO SHE
KNOWS WHEN SHE'S OVER
SPENDING!!
TRY TO TEACH HER TO RESPECT
THE MAN SHE MARRIED. THIS IS
WHO SHE IS SUPPOSE TO LOVE AND
STAND BY.. (NOT THE TWO OF YOU)
OR WAS IT EASIER FOR YOU TO
JUST GIVE HER WHAT EVER SHE
WANTED JUST TO KEEP HER QUIET!!!
NOW WE HAVE THREE TEENAGE
GIRLS AGES SIXTEEN YEARS OLD
WHO MAKE A BET TO SEE WHICH
ONE OF THEM CAN GET AN OLDER
MAN TO FALL IN LOVE WITH THEM
AND THEN JUST DUMP THEM!!!
THERE'S NO MONEY INVOLVED IN
THE BET, IT'S A GAME TO THEM,

PLAYING ONLY TO SEE WHAT KIND
OF FOOLS THEY CAN MAKE OUT OF
GROWN MEN BETWEEN THE AGES OF
TWENTY-ONE TO THIRTY-FIVE
YEARS OLD.
GOING TO BED WITH SOMEONE
THEY CARE NOTHING ABOUT IS NO
PROBLEM FOR THEM!!!
HOW COLD BLOODED CAN YOU BE
TO DO THIS TO ANYONE!!!!
YOU ONLY HAVE TO BE FEMALE
TO HAVE A COLD HEART!!!!
IF A WOMAN NEEDS A PLACE TO
STAY, SOMETHING TO EAT, A RIDE
SOMEWHERE, EXTRA MONEY,
SOMETHING TO DRINK, A NEW
DRESS.
NAME JUST ABOUT ANYTHING
THEY WANT AND A WOMAN WILL GO

TO BED WITH YOU FOR IT AND DOESN'T EVEN HAVE TO KNOW OR LIKE YOU!!!! WOMEN LIKE TO USE MEN'S ANIMAL LUST AGAINST THEM. AND MAN GIVES IN TO IT ALL THE TIME!!! (NOW STOP THAT WILL YOU)

LET THE WOMAN COME TO YOU DON'T GO CHASING AFTER HER.

ACT LIKE YOU COULD CARE LESS WHETHER OR NOT SHE'LL GO TO BED WITH YOU.

LET HER KNOW YOU'D RATHER WATCH FOOTBALL THEN LISTEN TO HER RATTLE ON.

TELL HER TO MAKE YOU SOMETHING TO EAT OR BRING YOU SOMETHING TO DRINK AND IF SHE DOESN'T LIKE IT SHE SHOULD MOVE ON, BECAUSE YOU DON'T HAVE TIME

FOR HER TO LEARN HOW TO TREAT
A MAN RIGHT.

TELL HER TO TAKE HER SILLY
REAR SOME WHERE ELSE.

YOU DON'T NEED SOMEONE
HANGING AROUND IF THEY DON'T
SERVE A PURPOSE AND THERE
PURPOSE IS TO MAKE YOU FEEL
SPECIAL AND IF THEY CAN'T DO
THAT THEN YOU DON'T NEED THEM.
THERE IS SO MUCH TOO TELL YOU
THAT I WOULD NEVER GET TO STOP
TYPING IF I TRIED TO GET IT ALL
DOWN ON PAPER AND IT WOULD
TAKE A YEAR TO READ!!!!

CHAPTER THREE

HOW TO GET YOUR MONEY

LETS SAY YOUR 25 YEARS OLD MAKING ABOUT $40,000 A YEAR. YOU RENT TO SAVE ON DOING ANY YARD WORK AND SO YOU DON'T HAVE TO WORRY ABOUT REPAIRS OR HAVE CUT GRASS OR SHOVEL THE SNOW. YOUR TOTAL EXPENSES FOR A YEAR ARE ABOUT $20,000 (CAR PAYMENT, RENT, INSURANCE, AND UTILITIES.) LEAVING YOU WITH ABOUT $6,500 IN SAVINGS AFTER TAXES. NOT BAD AND YOUR HAPPY. UH, OH A WOMAN ENTERS THE PICTURE!!!

AFTER DATING HER FOR ABOUT FOUR MONTHS SHE WANTS TO GET MARRIED!!!

SHE TELLS YOU, WE SHOULD GET A HOUSE. THE APARTMENT YOU LIVE IN IS TO SMALL FOR THE TWO OF YOU, AND SPENDING MONEY ON A MORTGAGE IS BETTER THEN SPENDING IT ON RENT. (YEA RIGHT).

THE HOUSE SHE PICKS OUT HAS A POOL AND THREE BEDROOMS IT'S FOR THE KIDS YOUR GOING TO HAVE.

NOW YOU NEED NEW FURNITURE AND NEW CURTAINS AND NEW RUGS, NEW WALL PAPER AND OF COURSE SHE NEEDS NEW CLOTHES!!!!

SO NOW YOUR PAYING A MORTGAGE AND PROPERTY TAX,

PLUS YOU HAVE YARD WORK TO DO,
A ROOF TO FIX AND LETS NOT
FORGET TO REPAIR THE POOL
FILTER, AND YOUR GETTING SUED
BY YOUR NEXT DOOR NEIGHBOR
THAT SLIPPED ON LAST YEARS ICE!!!!
YOU HAVE HAD YOUR CAR
REPOSSESSED, YOUR NOW DRIVING A
1987 CAR THAT WAS NEVER
MANUFACTURED. YOU PUT IT
TOGETHER FROM FIVE OTHER JUNK
CARS IN ORDER TO GET TO AND
FROM WORK!!! (MY MY).
YOU CALL YOUR CAR A
SUDACHEVFORDDOTSON.
NOW YOUR LOOSING ABOUT
$2,100.00 A YEAR!!!
AND YOUR BACK IS KILLING
YOU!!!! YOU HAVE BLISTERS EVERY

WEEKEND! YOU HAVEN'T SEEN YOUR FRIENDS IN MONTHS, AND THIS IS JUST THE FIRST TWO YEARS OF MARRIAGE!!!!

ISN'T WHAT YOU THOUGHT IT WAS GOING TO BE IS IT. WELL OF COURSE IT ISN'T "WHAT WHERE YOU THINKING CRAZY HUH" BUT DO YOU KNOW WHAT?? SHE'S HAPPY AS HELL!! (OH YEA).

LET'S LOOK AT IT FROM THE WOMEN'S POINT OF VIEW.

IF YOU LEAVE, SHE GETS THE HOUSE. YOU GET THE PAYMENTS. SHE GETS THE KIDS AND HALF YOUR SALARY. YOU GET TO CALL FOR PERMISSION TO VISIT YOUR OWN HOUSE.

YOU CAN SEE NOW HOW WOMEN CAN BE DECEITFUL.

SHE DOESN'T WANT TO LOSE OUT ON ANY OF THE MONEY!!!

WHEN THEY GET MARRIED AND WHEN THEY GET DIVORCED, THEY WANT ALL YOUR MONEY TO.

THEY WANT THE KIDS, BUT CAN'T AFFORD TO FEED THEM. SO THEY MAKE YOU PAY CHILD SUPPORT, AND THEN YOU HAVE TO DANCE TO THEIR TUNE JUST TO SEE THE KIDS.

WHEN SHE ASKED YOU TO TAKE THEM SOME WHERE.. SHE'LL NEVER GIVE UP ANY GAS MONEY!!

HERE'S I GUY THAT KNOWS WHAT HAPPENS AFTER DIVORCE. HIS NAME IS JOHN

HIS WIFE LEFT HIM FOR AN OLDER MAN WITH MONEY. NEVER GOT A DIVORCE BUT THEY DID HAVE A CHILD.

NOW I DON'T KNOW WHAT KIND OF LEGAL AGREEMENT THEY HAD BUT THIS DOESN'T MATTER.

JOHN NEEDED A RIDE TO THE BAY TO SEE HIS WIFE BECAUSE IT WAS HIS DAUGHTER'S BIRTHDAY AND HE NEEDED ME TO DRIVE CAUSE HE WAS TAKING A NEW BIKE AND HE ONLY HAD A SPORTS CAR.

AS WE WERE DRIVING HE SAID HE ALSO WAS GOING TO GIVE HIS WIFE $500.00 TO HELP WITH EXPENSE OF HIS DAUGHTER.

I SAID JOHN AREN'T YOU PAYING MONEY TO THE COURT.

HE SAID NO, HE SAID HE KEEPS
ALL THE CHECKS TO SHOW HOW
MUCH HE'S BEEN PAYING AND HIS
WIFE WENT ALONG WITH THIS
BECAUSE CHILD SERVICES WOULD
TAKE SOME OF THE MONEY. (YOU
SEE THEY WANT EVERY PENNY).
WELL NOW I TELL JOHN HE'S
CRAZY IF HE DOESN'T PAY IT TO THE
COURT ALL THE MONEY HE'S BEEN
GIVING HER WELL BE NOTHING
MORE THEN A GIFT.
NOW IF YOUR WIFE DECIDES TO
COME BACK AT YOU TWO OR THREE
YEARS FROM NOW WHEN THIS GUY
DECIDES IT TIME TO GET ANOTHER
YOUNGER GIRL AND YOU'RE WIFE IS
THROWN OUT AND THE ONLY PLACE
SHE CAN GET MONEY IS FROM YOU.

HE SAYS SHE WOULD NEVER DO
THAT. (OH YEA).
NOW I SAID ONCE BEFORE I DON'T
REPEAT A WARNING.
IT WAS THREE YEARS LATER AND
JOHN WAS GOING TO HAVE A PARTY
FOR THE OLD BUNCH THAT RAN
AROUND TOGETHER BACK IN THE
DAY.
I WAS WAITING FOR JOHN TO GET
READY AND AS I WAS DRINKING
SOME TEA I SAW A LEGAL LETTER
SITTING THERE WITH THE NOTICE
LYING OUT.
IT SAID THAT HIS WIFE WAS SUING
HIM FOR BACK SUPPORT AND THAT
HE OWNED $12,000 FOR 4 ½ YEARS.
JOHN HAD GIVEN HER OVER
$27,000 (TO BAD IT DOESN'T COUNT).

**JOHN SEE ME LOOKING AT THE
LETTER AND SAYS "JUST DON'T SAY
YOU TOLD ME SO. COLEMAN).
THIS IS WHY I WOULD SUGGEST!!!
(NOW LISTEN)
WHEN YOU FIRST GET MARRIED.
STAY IN THE APARTMENT THE FIRST
TWO YEARS. IT GIVES YOU A
CHANCE TO SEE IF THE
RELATIONSHIP WILL WORK.
(BEFORE YOU LOSE EVERYTHING)
YOU HAVE TO REMEMBER WHEN
YOU THINK THAT YOUR PUTTING UP
WITH ALL HER BAD HABITS ALL THE
TIME! SHE'S PUTTING UP WITH
YOURS.
YOU SEE THAT'S WHAT IT'S ALL
ABOUT LEARNING TO TOLERATE
EACH OTHER.**

THAT'S WHY IT SO IMPORTANT TO LOVE EACH OTHER TO START WITH.

NOW BACK TO THE FACTS.

IF YOU GIVE A GIFT TO A WOMAN WHO WILL NEVER GO OUT WITH YOU UNLESS THERE IS A FREE MEAL INVOLVED OR MOVIE OR ANYTHING ELSE SHE CAN GET FROM YOU.

BUT YOU CAN'T EVEN GET A KISS, EXCEPT TO KISS HER ASS!!

SHE'LL TAKE THE GIFT AND SAY TO HER FRIENDS AT WORK (THAT KNOW ALL ABOUT YOU) SHE DOESN'T WANT TO HURT YOUR FEELINGS.

BUT SHE DOESN'T MIND HURTING YOUR WALLET OR STRINGING YOU ALONG.

Ronald Jessy Coleman

SO WHEN YOU HAVE A WOMEN
THAT'S NEVER GOING TO KISS YOU
AFTER SEVERAL DATES, GET OUT.
YOUR LEAVING MIGHT MAKE HER
COME AFTER YOU AND IF NOT, THEN
YOU KNOW WITHOUT MAKING MORE
OF AN ASS OF YOURSELF.
THAT SHE DOESN'T REALLY CARE
ABOUT YOU.
NOW IF YOU HAVE A WOMAN
THAT'S NOT YOUR WIFE!!
SHE HAS DIFFERENT WAYS TO
TAKE YOUR MONEY!!
SHE'LL SUE YOU FOR THE TIME
SHE SPENT PUTTING UP WITH YOU
AND GET MORE THEN WHAT YOUR
WIFE WOULD HAVE GOTTEN,
BECAUSE YOUR WIFE WOULD HAVE

**TO SHARE THE MONEY WITH THE
LAWYER.**

**YOU'LL REMEMBER THE
LAWYERS, THEY WANT ALL YOUR
MONEY TOO. YOU WOULD THINK
ALL ATTORNEY'S WERE WOMEN!!!!**

**SHE MIGHT TRY TO BLACKMAIL
YOU FOR THE LIVE SEX ACTS YOU
TAPED WITH HER WHEN YOU WERE
STILL TOGETHER.**

**BY BLACKMAILING YOU SHE
WON'T HAVE TO SHARE ANY MONEY
WITH HER LAWYER!!**

**SHE MIGHT HIDE YOUR MOST
IMPORTANT PAPERS AND NOT TELL
YOU WHERE THERE AT.**

**SHE MIGHT COME BACK
SOMETIME AND ACT LIKE SHE
WANTS YOU BECAUSE SHE MISSES**

97

Ronald Jessy Coleman

**THE GREAT SEX YOU USED TO HAVE
WITH HER!!!
DON'T BE FOOLED SHE STOPPED
TAKING THE PILL AND SHE'S TRYING
TO GET KNOCKED UP SO SHE CAN
HAVE SOME LEVERAGE ON YOU
NEXT MONTH WHEN SHE GETS THE
TEST RESULTS BACK!!
THE GREAT SEX SHE'S TALKING
ABOUT IS THE SCREWING SHE ABOUT
TO GIVE YOU LATER!!!
ANOTHER GOOD REASON TO
PRACTICE SAFE SEX. (USE RUBBERS)
NOW HERE'S BOB A GUY THAT
CAN TELL YOU JUST HOW FAR YOU
CAN TRUST A WOMAN.
BOB HAD WORKED AT THE CAB
COMPANY WITH ME FOR ABOUT**

THREE YEARS. HE HAD A FAMILY WITH THREE BOYS.

HIS MARRIAGE STARTED TO FALL APART AND HE HAD TO MOVE AND PAY FOR HIS THREE CHILDREN.

WITH THIS ADDED COST OF LIVING BOB HAD TO FIND ANOTHER JOB THAT PAID MORE.

SO I HADN'T SEEN BOB FOR ABOUT NINETEEN MONTHS WHEN ALL OF A SUDDEN HE'S BACK.

BOB TELLS ME HOW HIS WIFE WAS LETTING HIM STAY WITH HER BUT HAD TO MAKE HIM MOVE OUT TO GIVE THE KIDS MORE ROOM. (Like he had a choice).

HE TOLD ME HOW HE LOOKED FOR SOME PLACE TO LIVE. HE SAID

HE SLEPT IN HIS CAR UNTIL HE
FOUND AN APARTMENT.
THERE WASN'T ENOUGH ROOM
FOR HIS STUFF AND HIM IN THE CAR.
BOB WAS ALSO WORKING PART-
TIME AS A BAR TENDER AT NIGHT.
THE BAR MAID THERE TOLD HIM
SHE HAD AN EXTRA ROOM HE COULD
STORE HIS STUFF IN AND HE COULD
SLEEP ON THE COUCH. SOUNDS
GOOD!!!!
BEWARE ANYTIME SOMETHING
SOUNDS GOOD AND A WOMAN IS
INVOLVED IN IT.
"CAUSE A WOMAN CAN TAKE THE
GOOD RIGHT OUT OF IT!!
BOB ASKED HER WHAT HER RENT
WAS AND PAID HER HALF OF IT,

**GIVING HER $200 FOR THIS MONTHS
RENT.**

**BOB STAYS HERE FOR THREE
MONTHS GIVING THE BAR MAID A
TOTAL OF $600.**

**NOW THE NEW JOB BOB HAD LAYS
HIM OFF AFTER 18 MONTHS.**

**BOB HEADS BACK TO THE
APARTMENT AND FINDS HIS MONEY
MISSING ALONG WITH HIS CD'S AND
PLAYER!!**

**AS BOB TURNS AROUND HE SEES
SOME LARGE MAN LOOKING AT HIM.**

**HEY WHAT ARE YOU DOING IN
HERE THE MAN ASKED BOB!!!**

**BOB SAYS I'M STAYING HERE
WITH ANNIE, AND I THINK SHE
STOLE MY MONEY, CD PLAYER AND
CD'S.**

WELL I'M HERE TO CHANGE THE LOCKS CAUSE ANNIE OWES THREE MONTHS RENT AND YOUR GOING TO HAVE TO LEAVE!!!!

SO BOB SAYS "SURE JUST LET ME GET MY OTHER STUFF TOGETHER."

THE LANDLORD TELLS BOB THE LEASE ANNIE SIGNED STATES WHEN YOU DON'T PAY YOUR RENT, ALL BELONGINGS IN THE APARTMENT ARE HELD TILL PAYMENT IS MADE.

NOW HE'S GOT NO JOB, NO MONEY, NO PLACE TO STAY, AND HAS NO STUFF. (my my my) SOUNDS GOOD RIGHT!!!

HOLD ON NOW THERE IS STILL MORE, YOU KNOW HE'S STILL STANDING!

SO BOB COMES BACK TO THE CAB COMPANY.

HE COMES INTO THE OFFICE AND ASKED TO USE THE PHONE TO CALL HIS EX!!!!

I ASKED HIM WHAT DOES HE NEED TO CALL HER ABOUT, HE SAYS BACK SUPPORT.

WELL, DON'T CALL HER, SHE'LL HAVE YOU ARRESTED!! SHE DOESN'T CARE IF YOU HAVE PROBLEMS.

HE TELLS ME I DON'T KNOW HIS WIFE SHE'S A GOOD WOMAN. (THERE'S THAT WORD GOOD AGAIN).

WHAT IS THIS MAN THINKING.

HE'S JUST BEEN SCREWED TO HIGH HEAVEN BY THIS GIRL ANNIE, AND HE THINKS HIS EX WIFE IS ANY DIFFERENT!!!!

WELL HERE COMES THE WAKE UP CALL!!!! Oh Yeah.

BOB TELLS HIS WIFE WHAT HAPPENED TO HIM AND TRIES TO ASSURE HER THAT IF SHE CAN GIVE HIM A FEW DAYS, HE'LL BE ABLE TO PAY HER THE SUPPORT MONEY HE OWNS HER!!!

HE GETS OFF THE PHONE AND SAYS "COLEMAN YOUR WRONG" HE SAID HIS EX-WIFE SAID POOR BABY, YOU COME RIGHT DOWN HERE, I'LL MAKE YOU SOMETHING TO EAT AND YOU CAN VISIT WITH THE KIDS!!!

HE BOUGHT IT HOOK, LINE, AND SINKER!! (my my)

I SAY WELL DON'T GET LOST ITS GOING TO GET BUSY HERE VERY SOON AND I'M GOING TO NEED YOU.

NOW AN HOUR AN A HALF LATER I CAN'T FIND DRIVER 36 "BOB"!!

THE PHONE IS RINGING, I PICK IT UP AND IT'S A RECORDING ABOUT A COLLECT CALL CLICK!! I HANG UP.

I'M TO BUSY ANSWERING OTHER PHONE LINES. AGAIN THE PHONE RINGS IT'S THE RECORDING AGAIN CLICK!!

NOW IT SLOWS DOWN AND THE PHONE RINGS, RIGHT IT'S THE RECORDING AGAIN!!!

WELL I HAVE TIME NOW SO I WAIT AND I HEAR A VOICE START YELLING "DON'T HANG UP DON'T HANG UP" IT'S ME BOB "DON'T HANG UP!!!

I SAY BOB WHERE THE HELL ARE YOU I NEED YOUR HELP AND IT

SOUNDS LIKE YOUR TALKING IN A
TOILET BOWL.

WELL,WELL BOB'S IN JAIL. HIS
WIFE HAD THE POLICE WAITING FOR
HIM WHEN HE GOT TO HER HOUSE!!
NO HOT MEAL, NO VISIT WITH THE
KIDS, AND LIKE THE LANDLORD
THEY WANT THE MONEY NOW!!!

GUYS THINK THAT BECAUSE A
WOMAN TALKS NICE TO THEM THAT
SHE'S NICE. WRONG THINK AGAIN.

IF A WOMAN IS TALKING NICE TO
YOU IT'S BECAUSE SHE WANTS
SOMETHING AND YOU MUST HOLD
THE KEY TO IT!!

LET ME GIVE YOU AN EXAMPLE
WHY YOU CAN NEVER TELL WHAT A
WOMAN IS THINKING.

I GOT MARRIED AND I WAS A DOG.

I STILL STAYED OUT WITH MY FRIENDS DRINKING ALL NIGHT.

NOW I COULD DRIVE AFTER DRINKING! IT WAS JUST SOMETHING I WAS ALWAYS ABLE TO DO.

MY FRIENDS KNEW THIS, SO I WAS ALWAYS DRIVING EVERYONE HOME IN THE MORNING.

I'D WOULD TAKE MY FIRST FRIEND HOME WHO LIVED IN A QUIET AREA THAT WAS STILL AND PEACEFUL UNTIL I PULLED UP.

THIS GUYS WIFE WOULD COME OUT YELLING AT THE TOP OF HER LUNGS CURSING TO HIGH HEAVEN AND THEN ALL THE LIGHTS IN THE NEIGHBORHOOD WOULD COME ON!!!

(my my)

NOW I GET TO MY OTHER FRIENDS HOUSE, AND HIS PILLOW WOULD BE ON THE FRONT LAWN HIS WIFE WOULD MAKE HIM SLEEP OUTSIDE!!!!

NOW I GET HOME AND MY WIFE WOULD HELP ME UP THE STAIRS PUT ME IN BED AND THEN GIVE ME A SPONGE BATH AND A GREAT HEAD JOB. (NICE HUH)

WELL THIS WENT ON FOR ABOUT A MONTH AND ONE NIGHT I TOLD MY FRIENDS THAT I WASN'T GOING TO STAY OUT ALL NIGHT WITH THEM ANYMORE.

ALL COME ON COLEMAN LET'S HANG OUT A LITTLE LONGER.

I SAID NO YOU GUYS STAY HERE BECAUSE YOUR MARRIED TO A

COUPLE OF BITCHES. I'M NOT
MARRIED TO A BITCH I GOT A GOOD
WOMAN AT HOME.

SO NOW I BECAME A GOOD GUY
WENT HOME RIGHT FROM WORK
AND STAYED THERE.

NOW THIS WENT ON FOR ABOUT A
WEEK OR TWO, BUT SOMETHING
WAS MISSING, WHAT'S UP.

SO I ASKED MY WIFE WHY SHE
WAS SO NICE TO ME WHEN I STAYED
OUT ALL NIGHT, AND NOW THAT I
COME HOME EVERY NIGHT SHE'S
NOT NICE TO ME ANYMORE.

SHE SAYS SHE DIDN'T KNOW
WHAT I WAS TALKING ABOUT.

SO I WENT THROUGH THE WHOLE
STORY ABOUT MY FRIENDS WIVES

**AND HOW SHE WAS THE ONLY ONE
THAT WAS NICE!!
NOW SHE STARTS TO LAUGH AND
SAYS, NICE TO YOU, NICE TO YOU.
YOU THINK I WAS BEING NICE TO
YOU. I WAS CHECKING TO SEE IF YOU
WERE EMPTY AND IF NOTHING
WOULD HAVE COME OUT, I WOULD
HAVE CUT IT OFF!!! OUCH.
SO REMEMBER YOU CAN NEVER
REALLY KNOW WHAT'S ON A
WOMAN'S MIND. (YOU KNOW THE
OLD SAYING) SUGAR AND SPICE AND
EVERYTHING NICE THAT'S WHAT
GIRLS ARE MADE OF**

INDEX TESTAMENT

..........{WHAT IT SHOULD SAY IS}
LEMONS AND LIMES WOMEN ARE
SOUR ALL THE

TIME..!!!
LOVING A WOMAN ISN'T
ENOUGH!!!

WORKING YOUR ASS OFF FOR
HER ISN'T ENOUGH
GIVING UP ALL YOUR FREE TIME
FOR HER ISN'T
ENOUGH!!!
ABANDONING YOUR FRIENDS
FOR HER ISN'T
ENOUGH!!

KISSING HER ASS FOR HER STILL
ISN'T
ENOUGH!!!
WOMEN WANT YOU TO PAY
TRIBUTE TO
THEM
LIKE FLOWERS, CANDY,
JEWELRY, OR A DINNER AND A
SHOW.!!

Ronald Jessy Coleman

WELL HERE'S MY TRIBUTE TO ALL WOMEN,,!!!! …

I WOULD LIKE TO PAY TRIBUTE TO
ALL THE MOTHERS AND WIVES OUT
THERE THAT STAY AT HOME TO
TAKE CARE OF THE KIDS OR DAD.
THIS IS ONE OF THE MOST
IMPORTANT JOBS THERE IS!!
THE FUTURE DEPENDS ON HOW
WELL WE DO WITH THE NEXT
GENERATION!! WHAT WE TEACH
THEM ABOUT LOVE, RESPECT, FAIR
PLAY, HOME AND FAMILY!!!
ONE OF THE MAIN REASONS WERE
HAVING SO MUCH TROUBLE WITH
THE YOUTH OF AMERICA TODAY IS.
NO ONE IS HOME WITH THE KIDS.
"TESTAMENT" IT HAPPENS WITH
DIVORCE TOO MANY TIMES!!

MEN SEE THEIR WOMAN CARING
MORE ABOUT THEIR CAREERS THEN
FOR THEIR FAMILY!!
THERE ARE TOO MANY WOMEN
LIBBERS OUT THERE TRYING TO
BRAIN WASH WOMEN INTO
THINKING THAT UNLESS A WOMAN
HAS A CAREER. THEY'RE A MAN'S
FOOL.
THEY TRY AND MAKE A MOTHER
OF TWO FEEL THAT SHE HAS NO
WORTH UNLESS SHE HAS A JOB.
THAT'S ALL THE WOMAN
LIBERATION MOVEMENT IS, A WAY
TO BRAIN WASH WOMEN INTO
THINKING THEIR WAY. (THE WRONG
WAY).
IF A MAN'S VIEW POINT IS
DIFFERENT. THEY SAY HE IS ONLY

**TRYING TO GET THE WOMAN TO BE
SUBSERVIENT!! (WHAT CRAP)
EVERYONE AT SOMETIME HAS
WANTED TO RUN AWAY FROM A
RESPONSIBILITY!!
YOU HAVE DONE THE SAME THING
WHEN YOU WERE IN SCHOOL AND
DIDN'T HAVE YOUR HOMEWORK
DONE OR THERE WAS A TEST
COMING UP!!!! Soooooooooo YOU
PLAYED SICK!!!!
THAT'S JUST WHAT THESE
WOMEN LIBBERS ARE DOING
RUNNING AWAY FROM THEIR
RESPONSIBILITY!!!!
BECAUSE THEY DON'T WANT TO
DO THEIR HOMEWORK!!!!
DID YOU EVER WONDER WHY
YOUR MOTHER REALLY DIDN'T**

THINK ANY OF THE GIRLS YOU KNEW
WERE NEVER GOOD ENOUGH FOR
YOU WHEN YOU WHERE YOUNGER!
THAT'S BECAUSE SHE HERSELF
KNEW YOU COULD "NEVER KNOW
WHAT A WOMAN WONT DO ". THE
PAIN
THIS BOOK IS WRITTEN IN HOPES
THAT SOME MEN MIGHT AVOID
BEING TAKEN IN BY A WOMAN.., AND
HAVING THEIR FEELINGS TORN
APART. TURNING THEM INTO MALE
PIGS THAT END UP MISTREATING
THE OTHER WOMEN THEY LATER
MEET IN THEIR LIFE BECAUSE OF
THEIR EARLIER MISTREATMENT BY
A WOMAN!!!
THE END

Ronald Jessy Coleman

TESTAMENT FROM PEOPLE WHO HAVE READ BOOK

CAB DRIVER SAYS WHAT HE LIKES MOSTABOUT THE BOOK IS THAT THE TRUTH ABOUT WOMEN HAS FINIALLY BEEN PUT IN PRINT

A STATE WORKER SAID THAT EVERYTHING IN THE BOOK WAS SO TRUE.

AN AFRICIAN WOMAN HERE TO VISIT SAID THE PART ABOUT ORGASMS IS SO TRUE AND IT IS IMPORTANT FOR A WOMAN, BUT A HORSE

A DISPATCHER SAID SHE PUT THE BOOK DOWN THREE TIMES BUT THOUGHT ABOUT WHAT SHE READ AND SAID TO HERSELF THAT'S TRUE AND THEN WOULD PICK IT UP AGAIN.

PRINTER FEMALE SALLY SAID THE ONLY WOMEN THAT WOULD BE OFFENDED BY BOOK WOULD HAVE TO HAVE A LOW I.Q.

Ronald Jessy Coleman

FEMALE WORKER ANN SAID SHE
GAVE IT TO HER BROTHER SO HE
MIGHT STOP LETTING WOMEN MAKE A
FOOL OF HIM ANYMORE

ABOUT THE AUTHOR

In 1968 I was a wild and crazy guy. I was called "king lizard" I had an apartment that had zebra stripes on the walls and a wet bar, it also had a parrot named cock. All the girls that went through my apartment loved this bird. We had a lot of wild parties. This is an apartment you would never let your mother see. It came to an end when the government came to tell me I was drafted. What a let down. Being overseas, I got a chance to see what European women were like, and they were more dangerous then American women were. Saying any thing just to get back to the states. When I got back to the real world I made a promise to myself to get every woman I could get in bed, and I did, having a partner for each time of the day. I had one for the night, one for in the morning, and one for lunch. I was doing it so much that I had to see a doctor who told me that he knew what I was up to, and I should be aware that I could kill myself if I didn't get some bed rest. Oh boy, that's just what I wanted. More bed time (oh, yea).